Troubling the Waters

Troubling the Waters

FULFILLING THE PROMISE OF QUALITY PUBLIC SCHOOLING FOR BLACK CHILDREN

Jerome E. Morris

Teachers College, Columbia University
New York and London

Published by Teachers College Press, 1234 Amsterdam Avenue, New York, NY 10027

Chapter 1 adapted and expanded from "Research, Ideology, and the *Brown* Decision: Counter-Narratives to the Historical and Contemporary Representation of Black Schooling," by J. E. Morris, 2008, *Teachers College Record, 110*(4), pp. 713–732. Copyright 2008 by Teachers College, Columbia University.

Chapter 5 adapted and expanded from "Can Anything Good Come from Nazareth? Race, Class, and African-American Schooling and Community in the Urban South and Midwest," by J. E. Morris, 2004, *American Educational Research Journal, 41*(1), pp. 69–112. Copyright 2004 by American Educational Research Association.

Chapter 7 adapted and expanded from "Forgotten Voices of African-American Educators: Critical Race Perspectives on the Implementation of a Desegregation Plan," by J. E. Morris, 2001, *Educational Policy, 15*(4), pp. 575–600. Copyright 2001 by Corwin Press.

Library of Congress Cataloging-in-Publication Data

Morris, Jerome E.
  Troubling the waters : fulfilling the promise of quality public schooling for black children / Jerome E. Morris.
       p. cm.
  Includes bibliographical references and index.
  ISBN 978-0-8077-5015-5 (pbk : alk. paper) — ISBN 978-0-8077-5016-2 (cloth : alk. paper)
  1. African American children—Education. 2. Educational equalization—United States. 3. Public schools—United States. I. Title.

  LC2771.M66 2009
  372.1829'96073—dc22

                                                                2009021894

ISBN: 978-0-8077-5015-5 (paper)
ISBN: 978-0-8077-5016-2 (cloth)

Printed on acid-free paper
Manufactured in the United States of America

16   15   14   13   12   11   10   09   8   7   6   5   4   3   2   1

Contents

Acknowledgments

Writing a book is not an individual process but one that requires the support and encouragement of many. Rather than at the end of the acknowledgments—as authors often do—I begin by thanking my lovely spouse, Mary, and our children, Amadi and Kamau, for their love and support in bringing this book into fruition. Mary has been there throughout the entire research and writing processes—joining me on some of my trips to St. Louis, and to the school and community in Atlanta to meet families and educators; she has also engaged me in deep intellectual discussions regarding the meaning of the research for everyday folks. When we moved to the metropolitan Atlanta area to be closer to one of the research sites, Mary supported my quest to complete the research study the right way. For her love and unwavering scholarly and emotional support, I thank her.

I would also like to thank my wonderful and very inquisitive children, Amadi and Kamau, who remind me every day that making changes in the world requires thinking "outside the box." Children are wonderful teachers and I am honored and thankful to play a significant part in shaping their minds and futures.

This book has been a collective effort—one that emanated from a deep understanding of African American people's belief in the power of education. It grew out of the constant prayers of my mother, Joann Steele Morris, and her hope that her seven children (Ronald, Richard, Kenneth, Michael, Maurice, Shelda, and me) would grow up to become good people. Although she is physically no longer with me, my mother's indomitable spirit inspires me to "keep on keeping on." Moreover, this book springs from the collective hope of my friends and neighbors in Central City, the public housing community in Birmingham, Alabama, where I was raised during the 1970s and 1980s, as well as the educators in the urban and predominantly Black K–12 public schools that I attended. Their support has sustained my personal and scholarly development and grounded me in the experiences of urban and low-income African American people that most social scientists only see from afar. Thus, I approached the research presented in this book with a nuanced understanding of Black people and institutions that is rarely captured in the sociological or educational literature on Black communities, families, and schools.

This book further grew out of the stories entrusted to me by the educators, families, and community members and presented throughout its pages. While conducting the ethnographic research in the schools and communities in St. Louis and Atlanta, I realized, even more so than previously, my responsibility in illuminating their experiences beyond the conventional narratives of urban Black families. I am indebted to the parents and educators charged with caring for and educating Black children because without them and their support, the book would never have been written.

Several individuals have provided much-appreciated intellectual and personal support over the years, and I extend sincere appreciation to Claire Smrekar, Ellen Goldring, Robert Crowson, David Bloome, and Yvonne Newsome for the opportunities earlier on to develop my skills as a social scientist. I owe a great deal of gratitude to Jeff Carr and Sam Brown for their camaraderie and for making my graduate school years in Nashville, Tennessee, a memorable experience. Jeff, the media scientist, reminded me of the importance of communicating with people so that they not only hear but also keenly listen to the information shared. Sam, through his commitment to teaching Black children about the field of science, generously gave of his time to the mentoring program for African American males that we lead.

Many thanks go to Derrick Alridge, my colleague and friend at the University of Georgia. I truly value our daily conversations about the field of African American Educational Studies and even more when these conversations include our dear friend Maurice Daniels, dean of the School of Social Work. To my colleagues in the College of Education and the Institute for Behavioral Research (IBR) at the University of Georgia, thank you for providing a supportive and engaging scholarly community.

Other individuals directly assisted me with the research or the editing processes. I would like to thank Bob Saffold, who participated in the early stages of the data collection in St. Louis, as well as Jamie Lewis and Kevin Williams, former graduate research assistants in the Social Foundations of Education program. Now Dr. Jamie Lewis and Dr. Kevin Williams, they assisted me with different phases of the research conducted in Atlanta. Preston Hughes and Stacy Gibbs, my two graduate students, also helped with the data collection and analysis. I especially thank Folami Prescott and Maude Glanton for lending a hand with early efforts to identify a research site in Atlanta. At the time, Folami was working as a researcher in urban education and Maude was a retired principal from the Atlanta Public School system. Pamela Denzmore and Vena Crichlow-Scales assisted with data collection and analysis. Pamela, who really made families feel comfortable in her presence, fell ill and passed away before this book could be completed; she is sorely missed and I give my condolences to her husband, Arthur.

I am thankful for assistance provided by Carla Monroe, who worked as a research scientist with me over the past few years on my other research project, which is a multiyear study of African American adolescents in Black suburbia in the South. Carla read the book in its formative stages and was insightful and critical in her feedback. For encouragement, reading every chapter during the summer of 2008, and challenging me to convincingly capture my thoughts on paper, I thank Wanda McGowan, a former dean at Vanderbilt University, and her spouse, Calvin.

In the broader academic community, a number of scholars have played a critical role in my thinking as reflected in this book. Michele Foster, a scholar and friend, generously gave of her time during the Atlanta research phase. She flew into the city to meet with some of the Atlanta educators presented in this book. Through her keen intellectual insights about the education of Black children, Michele has taught us that Black educators have voices that too often go unheard. Years ago, when I first broached her with some of the ideas presented in this book, Vanessa Siddle Walker generously offered feedback on some of my earlier manuscripts; I am very grateful. James Anderson's book *The Education of Blacks in the South*, demonstrated how Black people collectively worked to bring about schooling and literacy for themselves, even during the nadir of their experiences in the United States. The scholarly community's understanding of this sense of agency on the part of Black people, however, should not be consigned only to the historical narratives or the pre–*Brown v. Board of Education* era. It continues even today. This is part of what I have attempted to demonstrate in this book.

Kofi Lomotey's research on Black principals has been instrumental in my thinking. As readers will discover, principals played pivotal roles in creating a place for high academic performance and educational equity in three of the schools. Kofi has also been a friend. Although too numerous to mention, other scholars who have played a critical role in shaping my thinking include the late Asa Hilliard, Jomills Braddock, Carol Lee, Jacqueline Jordan Irvine, Kris Gutierrez, Jack Dougherty, Vivian Gadsden, William F. Tate IV, Garrett A. Duncan, Marion Orr, Elaine Brown, Carter Savage, Vivian Gunn Morris, Tondra Loder-Jackson, Lubna Chaudhry, Roslyn Mickelson, Gloria Ladson-Billings, Charles Payne, Geneva Gay, George Noblit, and Alton Pollard III.

Various phases of the research presented in this book have benefited immensely from seminars and presentations at the annual meetings of the

American Educational Research Association (AERA), American Sociological Association, and seminars at the following universities: Consortium on Chicago School Research (hosted by Edgar Epps) at the University of Chicago, the University of North Carolina at Chapel Hill, Michigan State University, the University of Memphis, Peabody College at Vanderbilt University, and Washington University in St. Louis. There are many more that I have not named; please charge this to my head, not to my heart.

I thank the various agencies and foundations that supported the research reported here, specifically the American Educational Research Association and the Spencer Foundation. Although they supported the research financially and through other means, the book does necessarily reflect the views of these foundations. The AERA and Spencer fellowship and grants allowed me to complete data collection and to work on my current research projects focused on Black adolescents in Black suburbia in the South. The Spencer Foundation, in particular, has been a wonderful source of support for social science research in education and takes a genuine interest in promoting expanded scholarly views of the schooling of Black children in urban and suburban areas of the United States.

Finally, my appreciation is extended to the editors at Teachers College Press, particularly Brian Ellerbeck, who believed in the project from the beginning and supported it along the way.

Introduction

Most contemporary social scientists who have written about *Brown v. Board of Education* (vis-à-vis public school desegregation) begin with the premise that the implementation of desegregation was inherently good for Black children. Since the *Brown* decision in 1954, this body of scholarship has disproportionately focused on the merits of racially balancing schools rather than, concurrently, investigating the extent to which Black children could receive quality and equitable schooling within either setting: (1) predominantly Black schools or (2) predominantly White or racially mixed schools.[1] By framing the discourse as an either–or argument (i.e., racially balanced and predominantly White schools are "good" and all-Black schools are inherently "bad"), scholarly inquiry up to this point has failed to address the merits and limitations of either choice for Black people.[2]

Moreover, while many of the scholars who embrace what may be considered a *desegregation-only* scholarly and policy paradigm provide dramatic accounts of urban schooling and vividly document the persistent structural, social, political, and economic inequities experienced by African Americans in urban schools, these scholars say very little about the role of African American culture, Black identity, and African American institutions in the schooling experiences and academic achievement of African American students. Consequently, in their allegiance to the ideals of integrated schooling, these scholars fail to critically assess how cultural processes and structures in predominantly White or racially mixed school settings often consign Black children to the academic margins within these schools and require that Black students tactfully negotiate their racial identities, often with dire academic consequences.

A major goal of this book is to provide a multifarious understanding of urban schooling by highlighting the precarious predicament facing urban low-income and working-class Black families when it comes to seeking quality schooling for their children. Situated within a political economy of urban schooling, the book underscores persistent structural inequalities affecting urban African American schooling, while simultaneously capturing African American agency and resilience as well as the role of

1

African American culture and institutions in the educational experiences and achievement of African American students.

A second and related goal is to critically assess both neoconservative and liberal ideologies that have permeated the political and scholarly discourse in the post–civil rights era, especially the idea that *racism is no longer relevant*. In doing so, the book builds on some of the arguments advanced by legal scholar Derrick Bell (1987, 1992, 2004), who highlights the permanence of race and racism in shaping the historical and contemporary educational conditions of African American people and the ways in which the implementation of *Brown* positioned Whites as primary beneficiaries and Blacks as secondary or incidental beneficiaries of reforms such as public school desegregation. Different from the many anecdotal accounts of urban Black schooling, the analyses and arguments presented in this book are informed by longitudinal and empirically based ethnographic and sociological research across four schools (two predominantly Black urban schools, a magnet school, and a predominantly White and suburban school) and two Black communities. One of the communities is in Atlanta, Georgia, and the other is in St. Louis, Missouri.

Furthermore, missing in contemporary discussions on African American education has been an equal treatment of both sides of what the preeminent scholar on race in the twentieth century, W. E. B. Du Bois, identified as the "separate Black school/mixed school" paradox (see Alridge, 2008; Du Bois, 1935). In 1935, Du Bois stated, "The Negro needs neither segregated nor mixed schools. What he needs is education. What he must remember is that there is no magic, either in mixed schools or in segregated schools." Greater scholarly and policy attention to improving predominantly Black schools is especially needed, given that more than 85 percent of the Black children in cities of the United States continue to attend schools that enroll a predominantly minority student population (National Center for Education Statistics, 2008). Many of these schools have student populations that are still more than 80 to 90 percent African American and low-income.

The Supreme Court's 2007 decision in *Parents Involved in Community Schools v. Seattle School District No. 1* and *Crystal D. Meredith v. Jefferson County Board of Education* to not allow school districts to use race to achieve racially balanced schooling was misguided. In these cases, the justices ignored the entire history of race and racism in U.S. society. However, while schools that enroll significant percentages of economically disadvantaged and minority students are often low-performing, the solution for rectifying the educational disparities facing Black children is not solely found in racially balanced or predominantly White schools either; in these schools Black children are often academically, culturally, and socially marginalized.

Unlike middle-class families (White and Black), poor and working-class African American families who reside in the central cities of the United States have few options in where they can live and where their children may attend schools. A cursory glance at urban school reform reveals that whatever the educational reform or policy—whether continued desegregation or the abandonment of desegregation altogether—poor Black children are often neglected and, consequently, continue to receive substandard schooling. The cases from Atlanta and St. Louis featured in this book represent vivid examples of this paradox.

THE CONTEXTS: ATLANTA, GEORGIA, AND ST. LOUIS, MISSOURI

Atlanta was the site of a famous test case for the quid pro quo of additional resources and Black control of schooling in exchange for the end of desegregation. The rejection of the desegregation plan in Atlanta in 1973, known by many as the Atlanta Compromise, included limited pupil integration, increased hiring of Black faculty, and the hiring of African American administrators for key leadership positions. This approach has come to be regarded by some observers and scholars as a failure of that particular strategy for ensuring equal education for urban and low-income African American children.

St. Louis, on the other hand, continued to pursue desegregation in its public schools. From 1983 to 1999, the city was the site of the nation's largest voluntary desegregation plan (officially called the St. Louis Interdistrict Transfer Plan). The plan provided African American parents with the option of sending their children to their assigned neighborhood schools, to magnet schools in the city, or to schools in one of 16 participating, predominantly White suburban school districts. Although parents were provided choices, many observers questioned the extent to which African American children academically benefited from the St. Louis plan.

This book captures how Black people in these two cities have not merely accepted the imposition of inequality; instead, they have displayed resilience in the face of formidable obstacles. To illustrate this resilience, the book highlights how two predominantly African American schools became renowned for educating predominantly low-income African American students. The campus grounds, the shiny hardwood floors, and the immaculate hallways inside of Fairmont Elementary School in St. Louis and Lincoln Elementary School in Atlanta defy the pervasive perceptions of beleaguered urban schools that are often depicted in media stories about African Americans. Unlike the picture painted by many scholarly accounts, the mostly African American educators at these schools have not given up on the school or, most importantly, the children. The educators in these schools have created what I define as *communally bonded* relationships with African American families and students.

The conceptualization of communally bonded schools (discussed later in the book) emerges from a synthesis of contemporary research on successful African American schooling and historical scholarship on schools that developed strong bonds with African American families and communities (Morris, 2004). Characteristics of communally bonded schools include: (1) The schools serve as pillars in the local Black communities; (2) the relationships between educators and African American students are intergenerational and cultural affirming; (3) the schools reach out to African American families and students; and (4) the principal serves as a bridge between the school and the local Black community and also ensures that students and teachers have the resources to succeed.

THE STUDIES

In each city, a low-income to working-class African community and the nearby school were the focal point. Methodologically, the focus on an African American community is akin to the studies of Black community life completed by scholars such as Du Bois (1899, 1902/1978a), Frazier (1939, 1957), Drake & Cayton (1945), and most recently, Pattillo-McCoy (1999). For example, intensive ethnographic data collection in St. Louis occurred from 1994 to 1997 (with additional data collection continuing in Fairmont Elementary School and the nearby community until 2006). The larger research project included ethnographic investigations of three types of public schools that were available to Black students in St. Louis under the desegregation plan: (1) a predominantly Black neighborhood school, (2) a predominantly White and suburban school, and (3) a magnet school.

The predominantly Black elementary school in St. Louis, Fairmont Elementary School, was selected for in-depth ethnographic study after repeated suggestions by African American educators (including principals, teachers, and district-level personnel) and community members. Fairmont Elementary School had a strong reputation for its academics and its connection with the local community. Using the community where Fairmont was located as a sample frame, a magnet school and predominantly White suburban school that enrolled children from the same community also served as ethnographic research sites. The community was a unit of analysis, thereby taking into account some of the effects of race and social class.

As in St. Louis, the school chosen in Atlanta was a predominantly African American school renowned for educating low-income African American children from the surrounding local area. Ethnographic and sociological research methods were employed to intensively investigate the school and community from 1999 to 2002, with additional data collection in the school and community occurring until 2005. Rather than present the two school ethnographies as separate studies, Lincoln Elementary School in Atlanta was juxtaposed with Fairmont Elementary School in St. Louis, and the overall findings were synthesized. The purpose of this approach was not to focus on what statisticians would call "outliers" in urban and predominantly Black schools, but to highlight counterexamples to the pervasive trend in urban school public districts as well as to address a significant omission in the scholarly understanding of contemporary urban and African American education.

ORGANIZATION OF THE BOOK

The book comprises three parts. Part I, "Visions and the City," consists of two chapters. Chapter 1, "Troubling the Waters: *Brown* and Black Folks' Shifting Visions of Quality Schooling," puts forth the argument that Black people's quest for quality schooling is not limited to the integration paradigm but can be placed within a complex ideological understanding of Black political thought.[3] Employing an African American cultural tradition of using metaphors to describe Black peoples' experiences, disguise hidden messages, and explain complex ideas and concepts, this chapter (1) provides a counternarrative to the master-narrative representation that Black people's ultimate quest was, and is, integrated schooling; (2) highlights African Americans' competing and sometimes conflicting support for desegregation; and (3) places African Americans' quest for quality schooling within a collective movement for Black educational freedom.

Chapter 2, "Making Central City Schools and Communities: The Indelible Influence of Race," provides a historical overview of Black people's quest for quality schooling in St. Louis and Atlanta as well as a comprehensive discussion of recent developments in the political economy of urban communities and schooling. Specifically noted are those forces that have contributed to the existence of central cities, communities, and schools that are overwhelmingly Black and low-income today. Some of these forces include: the Great Black Migration to urban centers in the 20th century; Whites' resistance to the mandates of *Brown* and subsequent flight into outlying suburbs; race-steering and other means of deterring Black families from moving into predominantly White communities; the White business elite's withdrawal of support from urban areas, especially when these cities became predominantly Black and began to elect Black mayors and superintendents as well as predominantly Black school boards (Henig, Hula, Orr, & Pedescleaux, 1999); and the decline in manufacturing jobs for low-skilled Black workers (Royster, 2003; Wilson, 1996).[4] Consequently, African American educational leaders in urban areas inherited a myriad of social and financial concerns. The chapter also describes the evolution of educational reforms in the cities that attempted to bring into reality *Brown*'s promises.

Part II, "Beyond Central Cities: In Search of *Brown*'s Second Promise," comprises two chapters and captures Black people's efforts to search within and beyond central cities to find quality schooling. Within a public school context, these choices have primarily been in the form of magnet schools and interdistrict transfer plans that allowed African American students to transfer into predominantly White suburban schools.

Chapter 3, "Whosoever Will, Can They Come? Black Families and Choices in a Magnet School," examines magnet schools as desegregation tools in the context of public school choice, specifically focusing on these schools as educational options for African American children. Using ethnographic research methods (in-depth interviews and observations), this chapter presents findings from an ethnographic investigation of a magnet school in St. Louis and illuminates the relationship between school personnel and Black families. The chapter highlights families' reasons for choosing the school, their experiences with school faculty and staff, and the dynamics of race and social class within the school. The school had a racially diverse faculty and staff, and major tensions existed in the school around race and the St. Louis desegregation plan. Moreover, this chapter particularly highlights the role of African American administrators in encouraging school personnel in this racially diverse school to more equitably serve African American students and their families.

Chapter 4, "Ambassadors or Sacrificial Lambs? Black Families and Students in a Suburban, White School," focuses on the experiences of Black families from the city of St. Louis who chose to send their children to a predominantly White suburban school (Spring Hill Elementary). In-depth interviews and rich descriptions of the everyday occurrences in the school elucidate Black parents' reasons for choosing to send their children to Spring Hill, constraints to Black parents' presence in the school, Black people's invisibility in the school, the disjuncture between Black parents and White educators' expectations of Black children, and other issues of race, social class, and identity.

Part III, "Quality Schooling in the New Black Metropolis; Possibilities and Dilemmas," contains three chapters. Chapter 5, "Out of Nazareth?

Promise in Central-City Schools," asserts that there is promise in some urban and predominantly African American schools today, just as there was in some all-Black schools during the segregation era.[5] This chapter describes how the scholarly community has neglected to study those urban and predominantly Black schools that successfully educated low-income Black students, thereby reinforcing the perception that nothing "good" can come from urban Black schools or from the communities where they are located. Chapter 5 focuses on two predominantly Black schools—one in St. Louis and the other in Atlanta—that were renowned for successfully educating low-income African American students. Given the demographic patterns in the United States in which so many low-income and ethnically diverse students learn in schools that are overwhelmingly one-race institutions, it is imperative to understand the circumstances under which some schools succeed with their students. By profiling these schools, the intent is to encourage more complex and multifaceted scholarly investigations of contemporary predominantly African American schools.

Chapter 6, "A Man Named Mr. Wooden: Generational Wisdom and the Care of Black Children," presents an intergenerational conversation with a family from a predominantly Black community in St. Louis. In the tradition of sociologists such as Elijah Anderson (1990, 1999), who relied on native informants, this conversation (occurring over multiple years) weaves together themes expressed throughout the book such as racial and economic changes within the community and school, gentrification, the Black school/mixed school paradox, and urban Black families and their quest to care for and educate their children.

Mr. and Mrs. Wooden have raised three generations of children (their daughter, her six children after she died, and three great-grandchildren). In the midst of the changes in the community, the school, and their family, Mr. Wooden's sacrifice and steadfastness demonstrate the resilience of some urban Black families and their deep commitment to caring for and educating Black children. The chapter presents life history interviews with Mr. Wooden and his granddaughter Renee, which provide a portrait of change in the community and school through the eyes of a family that has been residing in the same house since 1957. After graduating from college in December 2005, Renee enrolled in graduate school in 2007.

Chapter 7, "Voices in the Wilderness: Black Educators on School Reform," brings forth the voices of a group of professionals who have been ignored in historical and contemporary policy debates on how to improve the education of Black children. Based on in-depth interviews with Black educators in St. Louis and Atlanta across the four different schools, the chapter highlights these educators' perspectives on the merits and limitations of racially balanced schools as a method of educational reform; it also discusses the manner in which they, as a group of professionals, as well as Black institutions, have been negatively viewed in the context of this reform. The insights suggest the need for policy makers to also include the voices of Black educators when framing educational policies intent on improving African American children's education.

Chapter 8, "Fulfilling the Promise of Quality Schooling for Black Children," synthesizes the major themes of the book into a cogent discussion of the implications of the findings for theory, research, policy, and practice. The chapter places the empirical findings within the context of recent discourses on race, racism, and social-class inequalities in schools and U.S. society. Specifically highlighted are recent trends in urban areas, such as gentrification and the consequences for urban families and schools, policy discussions related to *No Child Left Behind* (*NCLB*), the academic achievement gap, charter schools, magnet schools, vouchers, and homeschooling. The chapter describes those factors across various school contexts that support and hinder African American students' educational and social development. Yet, given the prevalence of predominantly Black schools in urban areas, *communally bonded schools* are put forth as a conceptual—but pragmatic—framework for developing stronger connections (i.e., social capital) among existing urban schools and African American families and communities. Improving the schools where African American children attend is important, given the entrenched nature of racial segregation in communities—not just schools—across the United States, racial and demographic shifts across the United States, the inequities that African American children continue to experience in schools that are desegregated on the surface but segregated within, and the Supreme Court's recent decision against the use of race to promote public school desegregation.

Finally, to aid in the overall flow and readability of the book, an appendix provides a detailed overview of the methodologies used in the empirical works described. The book relies heavily on ethnographic research methods, and the appendix highlights the intersection of the researcher's role within the research process and the various measures taken to minimize the limitations.

SCHOLARLY APPROACH

I am a social science researcher whose research focuses on the sociology and anthropology of education and examines the intersection of race and social class with social and educational policies. Like many of the social scientists who have investigated the benefits of racially balanced school contexts, I recognize the value of children from diverse ethnic and social-class backgrounds attending schools together. But the scholarly community also needs to critically examine the educational marginalization of Black children in diverse school contexts.

One of the most troubling matters is the second-generation segregation experienced by Black students who attend racially desegregated schools (Meier, Stewart, & England, 1989; Mickelson, 2001; Tatum, 1997). In comparison to their White peers in the same school, Black students are more likely to be overrepresented in lower academic tracks and special education (Braddock, 1989; Mickelson, 2001; Oakes, 1985), underrepresented in gifted education (Ford & Harris, 1999; Morris, 2002), and disproportionately disciplined (Monroe, 2005; Morris & Goldring, 1999). Many of the reasons for inequities facing Black students, particularly Black males (as the 2008 events surrounding "Jena Six" illustrate), have been traced to subjective reasons, which is less true for White students (Ferguson, 2000; Monroe, 2005).

It is true that persistent structural inequalities have adversely affected the quality of schooling received by urban and low-income Black children today. However, it is not instructive to address these inequalities primarily by presenting Black people and their institutions in deficit-ridden and pathological ways. Growing up in a public housing community and attending urban and predominantly Black schools in Birmingham, Alabama, during the 1980s has shaped my understanding of the multifarious nature of urban Black schools, communities, and families. As a researcher who employs thorough research methods, my identity and professional and personal background enhance the analyses and arguments in this book.

Methodologically, I balanced my perspective by chronicling my perceptions of the events in the schools and communities, maintaining a degree of professional distance as a researcher, and by keeping an "objective eye" throughout the research process (also see Alridge, 2003; Milner, 2007; Tillman, 2002).

As this volume argues, social scientists, policy makers, educators, and families have to develop a multifaceted approach toward improving the schooling of urban Black children and, consequently, their overall life chances. The perilous path of embracing only one particular ideology or framework must not continue. That is the soul of this book.

PART I

Visions and the City

CHAPTER 1

Troubling the Waters: *Brown* and Black Folks' Shifting Visions of Quality Schooling

Wade in the water
Wade in the water, children
Wade in the water
God's gonna trouble the water

Through the use of metaphors to disguise their meaning, Negro Spirituals such as *Wade in the Water* were often used by enslaved Black people as a secret mode of communication (Cone, 1991; Jones, 1993). On their many journeys on the *Underground Railroad*, Black abolitionists such as Harriet Tubman sang *Wade in the Water* to warn escaping Black people to change course by wading through the waters. Traveling through and troubling the waters prevented dogs and slave catchers from picking up Black peoples' scent. Though doing so was uncomfortable, unpredictable, and unsafe, Black people had to trouble the waters in their movement toward freedom.

Building on African Americans' use of metaphors to convey deeper messages and information, this chapter "troubles the waters" in relation to the conventional depiction of Black people's interpretation of quality schooling for their children. This multifaceted analysis of Black people's various visions of *Brown v. Board of Education* may have implications for how policy makers, school districts, and educators embrace their charge to educate urban and low-income African American children today.

In many urban public school districts of the United States today, African American students continue to represent the overwhelming majority of the student population, with some cities enrolling student populations that are more than 80 to 90 percent African American.[1] Given the contemporary social context in which many low-income African American students are schooled, how can the promises of *Brown*—that is, its promise of racially integrated schools and its promise of a quality education for

13

Black children—become realized more than 50 years after the decision was handed down?

The passage of *Brown v. Board of Education of Topeka, Kansas* on May 17, 1954, arguably the most significant U.S. Supreme Court case of the 20th century, brought about a renewed sense of hope for Black people then— much as did the 2008 election of Barack Obama as the president of the United States. Unfortunately, the hope that was so luminous then faded away in only a few years because, in many places, this court ruling was not implemented until more than 15 years later. When compelled to implement the court case, many White people ensured that the implementation did not threaten their superior social status. While numerous scholarly conferences, events, celebrations, and publications emerged from the 50th anniversary celebration of *Brown* in 2004, poor Black children throughout the urban areas of the United States continued to wait for *Brown* to deliver on its promise of quality schooling.

BROWN'S VISION: EXTENDING BEYOND EDUCATION

In revisiting *Brown* and Black people's shifting visions of quality schooling, it is imperative to highlight the significance of this court case beyond schooling. *Brown* was part of a broader legal strategy initially led by Charles Hamilton Houston, who laid the legal foundation for the case but passed away before *Brown* was argued. Consisting of Thurgood Marshall, Constance Motley Baker, and Robert Carter, the *Brown* legal team's ultimate goal was to dismantle legalized segregation in society and education—and to create a nation in which all were equal under the law (Ogletree, 2004). Therefore, schools became a part of the strategy of this dismantling of contrived barriers, not merely for educational purposes but also for broader social change within the United States.

To accomplish this, however, Black lawyers had to mount a legal argument against the 1896 Supreme Court decision *Plessy v. Ferguson*, which stated that there was no violation of the equal protection clause of the Fourteenth Amendment to the Constitution so long as equal facilities existed for Black and White people. For more than half a century after its passage, the *Plessy* decision etched in stone the notion of "separate but equal." The *Brown* legal team had to attack an entrenched system that had a long history of Black subordination and a national history that included the complete disenfranchisement—politically, socially, economically, and educationally—of enslaved African people (Anderson, 1988; Smith, 1999). Other than segregated public parks and water fountains, schools were the most visible manifestation of Jim Crow—the symbol of legalized segregation in public facilities predicated on relegating Black people to second-class citizenship. Therefore, the strategy by the *Brown* legal team to mount the challenges to Jim Crow laws via public schools was logical from a legal perspective.

Contemporary scholarly discussions of "the promises of *Brown*" usually focus on achieving racially balanced schooling rather than also considering the extent to which Black children might receive quality schooling across school contexts—whether predominantly Black, predominantly White, or integrated (Philipsen, 1994). Some scholars have spent their entire academic lives researching the benefits of desegregation and often frame Black people's ultimate educational goal throughout history as a quest for their children to attend integrated schools, which is far from accurate.[2]

The neoconservative discourse, on the other hand, by putting forth the argument that racism is no longer relevant, asserts the need to abandon policy efforts that focus on creating greater racial and social-class equality. The most contentious of these policies have been affirmative action and public school desegregation mandates. Personified by individuals such as Ward Connerly, embracers of this view ignore how entrenched racist structures—during enslavement, Jim Crow, and even up to the present—have created the present social, political, and economic system that results in disparities and disadvantages. They often argue that no one is committing racist acts toward Black people and that White people are now being discriminated against. In fact, this was the rationale presented by the White parents in the Louisville school desegregation case that was decided by the Supreme Court in 2007. Yet this neoconservative view refuses to understand that there does not have to be a racist actor in order for there to be a racist action. "Racism, however, is as much a product of systems and institutions as it is a manifestation of individual behavior. Indeed, structural arrangements produce and reproduce racial outcomes and can reinforce racial attitudes" (Powell, Jeffries, Newhart, & Stiens, 2006, p. 65).

Rather than acknowledge how White racism, discrimination, and prejudice continue to adversely affect the contemporary experiences of African Americans in a range of areas, conservatives and neoconservatives often focus on the failings of Black people and their culture as the major factor affecting Black educational and social upward mobility. Furthermore, such perspectives, although arguing for African Americans to assume "greater responsibility" for their predicament, abhor the idea of African American people embracing culturally affirming and self-determined frameworks in the process.

Many within the educational research and the larger social science communities are correct in their assessment of the flawed analysis in the conservative and neoconservative arguments. Yet a corresponding critique of the *desegregation-only* paradigm is also noticeably absent. This paradigm, although well intentioned, ignores the significance of African Americans' experiences, culture, and institutions in the larger quest for educational equity and academic achievement.

AFRICAN AMERICANS' CURRENTS AND COUNTERCURRENTS ON ALL-BLACK AND INTEGRATED SCHOOLING

Contrary to the conventional view of their educational quest, Black people did not embrace the one-dimensional desire for integrated schooling that has often been portrayed by some scholars who have written about this pivotal Supreme Court case and its implications for public schooling. To illustrate this point, when some all-Black schools were targeted for closure upon the implementation of desegregation, African American communities protested the decisions. David S. Cecelski's (1994) book *Along Freedom Road* chronicles Black communities' struggles to preserve their schools. Among their efforts, Black students and families in Hyde County, North Carolina, engaged in forms of civil disobedience such as sit-ins and marches, while simultaneously withdrawing their children from the schools to be educated at home. One of the most sustained civil rights protests in North Carolina, the school boycott was a microcosm of African Americans' resistance to the closing of Black schools and the dismissal or demotion of Black educators.

However, in *Brown v. Board of Education: A Civil Rights Milestone and Its Troubled Legacy*, James T. Patterson (2001) presents a one-dimensional portrait of African Americans' struggle for quality schooling as one that primarily focused on the pursuit of integrated schooling rather than a movement that was also inclusive of African Americans' desire for equal resources for their existing all-Black schools. Patterson ignores the fact that many African Americans valued their Black schools—albeit segregated— and he fails to critically assess how Black people have always been concerned about the cultural ramifications for their children if they were to attend predominantly White schools.

As scholars such as Dougherty (2004) have noted, there was "more than one struggle" for quality schooling for Black people, both before and during the modern civil rights movement. Rather than as a one-dimensional interpretation of *Brown*, the push by Black people for integrated schooling should be viewed within the contours of Black political thought, which encompasses multiple ideologies (of which integration represents only one) and is influenced by geography, time, and Black people's particular experiences. For example, Michael Dawson (2001), a political scientist who has written extensively about Black political thought, further illustrates this point in *Black Visions: The Roots of Contemporary African-American Political Ideologies.*

Dawson elucidates six ideologies embraced by Black people: radical egalitarianism, disillusioned liberalism, Black Marxism, Black conservatism, Black feminism, and Black nationalism.[3] When Black people departed from traditional integrationist ideology, according to Dawson, they often embraced elements of disillusioned liberalism, which maintained skepticism toward White people's true efforts to create a truly egalitarian schooling environment for Black children.

A number of scholars (Bell, 2004; Dudziak, 2000; Klarman, 2002) note how the *Brown* decision was not solely about protecting the rights of African Americans; it was also about the United States positioning itself as a "champion of democracy" in the world during the Cold War era. The United States would appear hypocritical to the rest of the world if it legally continued the disenfranchisement of African American people. Derrick Bell, a former NAACP (National Association for the Advancement of Colored People) Legal Defense Fund lawyer, argued that desegregation measures ignored the fact that legalized segregation was about maintaining White control of education. In *Silent Covenants*, Bell (2004) echoes the sentiments of Dudziak (2000) and Klarman (2002). Bell terms this an interest convergence covenant: a decision in which Black peoples' "rights are recognized and protected when and only so long as policymakers perceive that such advances will further interests that are their [Whites'] primary concern" (p. 49).

Some African Americans embraced elements of Black nationalist thinking—a belief in the maintenance and support of Black institutions in a manner that reaffirmed Black culture and identity. Black nationalist thought in education was best exemplified by Malcolm X, a spokesperson for the Nation of Islam; it provided the ideological foundation that guided many of the schools started by the Black Panther Party and by individuals affiliated with the Council of Independent Black Institutions (CIBI).[4] Today, many independent Black educational institutions in the United States reinforce African and African American culture, identity, and history through all facets of the school's curriculum (Shujaa & Afrik, 1996).

Throughout their experiences in the United States, Black people have been ambivalent about whether to send their children to all-Black schools or predominantly White schools. For example, in Boston in the late 18th century, Black children were allowed to attend the Boston public schools, but few parents enrolled their children because of prejudice on the part of White teachers. In 1787, the Revolutionary War veteran Prince Hall petitioned the Massachusetts legislature for an "African" school because of Black students' mistreatment in integrated schools. A school was later opened for Black students in Hall's son's home and separate schools were later established for the Black students in the city (Bell, 2000; Hall, 1787/1951). For Black families during this time, educational equality was associated more with attendance at Black schools than at integrated schools.

However, the idea that separate schooling was better for Black children changed with time. Later, some of the Black parents in Boston protested the actions of the Boston public school system, which segregated Black children from White children. In 1849, a group of Black parents, in *Roberts v. City of Boston* (1850), fought for integrated education because they felt that separate tax-supported schools were inferior in quality. In this court case, abolitionist and attorney Charles Sumner—aided by Robert Morris, one of the first Black attorneys—argued that separated Black schools were inferior in quality and created a feeling of inferiority in Black students (see also Bell, 2000).

Black people's efforts to ensure quality schooling for their children transcend time and place and have changed over time. For instance, Dougherty (2004) captures the Milwaukee Black community's 60-year quest for quality schooling for their children (1930–1990). In the 1930s, the focus was more on increasing the numbers of Black teachers for Black children; the proponents of this model did not equate Black schools with inferior teaching. During the 1950s and 1960s, integration predominated as the main thrust within the movement, whereas the 1980s and 1990s witnessed the emergence of school vouchers and Afrocentric schools, respectively.

These multiple struggles by Black people for quality schooling demonstrate the challenges that they have historically faced. Yet Black people have always understood the precarious predicament of favoring one position over the other. If one pushed for Black children to attend schools with White children, the chance of losing community control of schools was great, as was the possibility of Black children and their culture being totally ignored in the curriculum and the culture of the school. If children were relegated to all-Black schools, concerns remained about the lack of resources, lack of exposure to rigorous academic curriculum, and lack of facilities.

While the conventional view suggests that Black people overwhelmingly believed that integrated schools could lead to effective schooling for their children, such a view has not been unanimous over the history of Black people's experiences in the United States or among African American activists, leaders, and scholars such as W. E. B. Du Bois, Mary McLeod Bethune, Zora Neale Hurston, and Dr. Martin Luther King Jr. These individuals were deeply committed to Black freedom and equal participation in the broader U.S. society.

For instance, W. E. B. Du Bois (1935) vehemently challenged the NAACP's integrationist approach toward creating educational equality for African Americans. Ideally, Du Bois—arguably the most influential scholar on race and society of the 20th century—supported the "mixed" or integrated school as the optimal setting for any child. However, given the social conditions during the time in which he was writing, Du Bois had little confidence that such schools would be in the best interest of Black children— emotionally or educationally. Consequently, Du Bois (1935) argued that separate schools for "Negro" children should also be considered in Black people's quest for quality schooling:

> The Negro needs neither segregated nor mixed schools. What he needs is education. What he must remember is that there is no magic, either in mixed schools or in segregated schools. A mixed school with poor and unsympathetic teachers, with hostile public opinion, and no teaching of truth concerning Black folk is bad. A segregated school with ignorant placeholders, inadequate equipment, poor salaries, and wretched housing is equally bad. Other things being equal, the mixed school is the broader, more natural basis for the education of all youths. It gives wider contacts; it inspires greater self-confidence; and suppresses the inferiority complex. But other things seldom are equal, and in that case, Sympathy, Knowledge, and Truth, outweigh all that the mixed school can offer. (p. 335)

Du Bois once fervently believed in integration and was one of the founders of the NAACP, but he broke from the organization in 1934 because of ideological differences.[5] Du Bois disagreed with the decision by NAACP leaders Walter White and Roy Wilkins to put their resources behind interracial efforts rather than also advocating for the support of Black educational institutions. In his analysis of the separate Black school/mixed school paradox in the 1935 article, Du Bois raised a major point about the significance of Black culture and social support in the educational experiences of Black students (see also Alridge, 2002, 2008). Although all-Black schools—because of racist practices and policies from White school, district, and government officials—lacked the necessary resources to optimize Black students' education, Du Bois asserted that Black schools employed educators who were committed to educating Black children. Furthermore, he concluded that the cultural and psychological sustenance of Black schools and teachers, for Black children, should not be ignored in the overall effort to eradicate legalized segregation in U.S. society.

To intellectually frame their scholarship, a number of contemporary scholars have employed Du Bois's intellectual insights, particularly his analysis of race and the color line in U.S. society. Examples include: Michael Eric Dyson (1996), Nell Irving Painter (2002), and Amy Stuart Wells and Robert L. Crain (1997). As social scientists who have focused greatly on the value of desegregated school contexts, Wells and Crain, in particular, appear to have selectively appropriated Du Bois's thought on the separate Black school/mixed school paradox, thereby leading the reader to infer that Du Bois supported only the mixed school model rather than also advocating for separate Black schools that successfully educated Black children. They unambiguously address integration as a core value, which guides the way they frame their argument and describe the schooling experiences of Black students in the predominantly White and Black schools in St. Louis.[6]

It is important to place Du Bois's discussion of the separate Black school/mixed school paradox within a larger social context of the debate among leaders of numerous Black organizations—beyond the NAACP—about whether to pursue integration or to support autonomous Black communal institutions. For example, Paula Giddings (1984) cogently captures the internal and external tension among influential Black leaders such as Mary McLeod Bethune (1875–1955) regarding the support of separate Black institutions. Although she had a delicate balancing act because of the support she received from White philanthropists for her school and organizations, Bethune resonated with Du Bois's beliefs by advocating for separate Black institutions (Giddings, 1984).

An educator, civil rights activist, and trusted adviser to President Franklin D. Roosevelt, Bethune publicly championed interracial cooperation in society, simultaneously working to create and sustain Black educational institutions such as Daytona Normal and the Industrial Institute for Girls (which later became Bethune–Cookman College) as well as the Association for the Study of Negro Life and History (whose president she served from 1936 to 1951) (Alridge, 2008; Giddings, 1984; Loder-Jackson, in press; McCluskey & Smith, 1999). However, in 1935 Bethune supported the withdrawal of the National Association of Colored Women from the predominantly White National Council of Women, eventually advocating the formation of a separate and all-Black women's organization. Bethune said that the predominantly White women's organization had "forty three organizations with only one Negro organization and we have no specific place on their program" (quoted in Giddings, 1984, p. 212). Always judicious in her use of words so as not to alienate her White benefactors, Bethune further noted that "we need an organization to open new doors for our young women [which] when [it] speaks its power will be felt" (quoted in Giddings, 1984, p. 212). In 1935, Bethune founded the National Council of Negro Women, whose mission was to serve as an "organization of organizations" that represented the concerns of Black women.

The noted anthropologist, novelist, and folklorist Zora Neal Hurston (1955) expressed similar sentiments as Du Bois, which were dismissed by many African American civil rights leaders because of her support for conservative politicians and publications.[7] Furthermore, the foremost champion of the modern civil rights movement, Dr. Martin Luther King Jr., deeply understood the value of sustaining Black educational institutions for Black people—institutions that were key in promoting a sense of pride among Black people. During one of his earlier statements on integration in society, King had the following to say in 1959 to two Black teachers who taught at the all-Black George Washington Carver High School in Montgomery, Alabama:

> I am for equality. However, I think integration in our public schools is different. In that setting, you are dealing with the most important asset of an individual—the mind. White people view Black people as inferior. A large percentage of them have a very low opinion of our race. People with such a low view of the black race cannot be given free rein and put in charge of the intellectual care and development of our boys and girls.[8]

Yet King also realized that legalized segregation was more about maintaining White supremacy over Black people than about supporting Black institutions. In his support for the eradication of legalized school segregation and the promotion of racial equality, however, King did not hold the view that Black educational institutions would be unnecessary in the quest for educational equality. For him, they were valuable for Black children's identity and sense of pride.

While the *Brown* decision dismantled legalized segregation in public schools, how to implement this court case would be another matter. *Brown II*, decided in 1955, stated that "all deliberate speed" should be employed in adhering to the mandates of *Brown*. However, *Brown II* gave White resisters the opportunity to mount strategies to delay or circumvent the implementation of *Brown* (Ogletree, 2004). In essence, implementation was left in the hands of local White school boards. One of the most ardent supporters of desegregation as the means to implement *Brown* was Derrick Bell, then a civil rights attorney working for the NAACP's Legal Defense Fund and later a law professor at Harvard University. Bell supervised more than 300 desegregation cases.

But after having witnessed the loss of Black schools as key institutions for Black children, families, and communities, as well as the many perils faced by Black children when school systems were ordered to comply with the mandates of *Brown*, Bell later changed his views. He argued that desegregation measures throughout the United States ignored the fact that legalized segregation was about maintaining White control of education. He noted that if a desegregation plan inconvenienced and threatened White people and their superior social status, then implementation would occur in a way that ensured that White people still controlled public education (Bell, 1987). In further writings, Bell (1992, 2004) asserts the following: (1) Racism is permanently etched in the social and cultural order of American society; (2) significant progress for African Americans is achieved only when the goals of Blacks are consistent with the needs of Whites (i.e., there is an *interest convergence*); and (3) Whites will not support civil rights policies that appear to threaten their superior social status.[9] Bell's analyses of race and racism are echoed in some of the empirical findings presented in this book.

Mrs. Woodson, an African American principal at Denson Magnet School, a racially diverse school in St. Louis, noted that historically, equality of education was more about Black people taking pragmatic steps to ensure that their children would have some semblance of an equitable education. From her perspective, Black children benefited only when White people take actions to make sure that their children became the primary beneficiaries:

> The focus of *Brown* was the right to go where you wanted to go. Many times, Black children had to leave their neighborhoods and attend schools in other neighborhoods. People were talking about equality. Before desegregation, they were busing Black children to overcome crowding. It was not my experience that they had all of the things in South St. Louis that people talk about. I've never been a proponent of sending Black children to sit in classrooms with White children. I've never been a proponent of putting Black children on the bus. I did not become a teacher with the goal of teaching in South St. Louis [where a greater percentage of White students attend public schools]. . . . Yes, people do take care of their own [children]. Black people wanted a decent education. I've got to make sure that my children get it because they [White people] are not going to deprive their children.[10]

On the other hand, Mr. Miles, a teacher at Fairmont Elementary School, an all-Black neighborhood school in St. Louis, believed that racial balancing was important because of the exposure it provided children from various racial and ethnic backgrounds.

You know, it [desegregation plan in St. Louis] is not a total waste. It's done some good; there are problems with it, but it has done some good. I think that a lot of children, if the children are not bused out there [to the predominantly White suburban schools], a lot of times they'll never get to mix with the other people, with the other races. I think they need that, because you need to learn how other people react to different things.

As the excerpts from Mrs. Woodson and Mr. Miles illustrate, Black people's perspectives on quality schooling and the racial balancing of public schools reflect multiple visions, each with its own merit. In their responses, each educator understood the precarious predicament by favoring one position over the other. Mrs. Woodson, the principal of a diverse magnet public school in St. Louis, was very skeptical about the true intent of the racial balancing of public schools but was pragmatic in ensuring that Black children received some resources. On the other hand, Mr. Miles, a teacher at an all-Black public elementary school in St. Louis, realized that public schools remained one of the last places where many children would get a chance to be around children from other races. For him, this, too, should be an educational and social goal of public schooling.

Thus African Americans' quest for quality schooling is not limited to one particular ideology. It is part of a longer tradition within the Black freedom struggle against oppression that Vincent Harding refers to metaphorically as "the river." As Harding notes (1981), rivers are "sometimes powerful, tumultuous, and roiling with life; at other times meandering and turgid" (p. xix). Just as rivers are defined as much by their countercurrents as they are by their other features, African Americans' enduring quest for quality schooling has been characterized by multiple, competing, and sometimes conflicting ideologies. And just as a river is made up of many streams, these various Black ideologies represent African Americans' collective surge toward educational freedom.

CHAPTER 2

Making Central City Schools and Communities: The Indelible Influence of Race

The schools in the inner cities of the United States do not enroll an overwhelming majority of Black and low-income students by chance. Up until the early 1960s, many of today's urban and predominantly Black schools were once predominantly White schools. And often, Black children were prevented from enrolling in these schools. Moreover, many of the public housing communities in these central cities were originally created for poor and working-class Whites after World War II, particularly for those who could not yet afford to purchase homes.[1] As a result of African Americans' demands for decent housing, federal housing policies later opened up public housing communities to poor Black people who had been systematically excluded from decent housing altogether. Eventually many communities in the central cities of the United States became the home for thousands of low-income Black families during the 1970s, 1980s, and 1990s.

By the late 1960s, African Americans had migrated in large numbers to urban areas and become a predominantly urbanized population. Prior to this time, most African Americans had resided in rural communities in the South. For instance, by 1970, 60 percent of African Americans lived in central cities of the United States (Jones & Jackson, 2002). This migration to the city has been attributed partly to the "Great Black Migration" in which African Americans left the South en masse and moved to northern metropolises, as well as African Americans' migration out of the rural South to urban centers within the South.

In addition, a pattern of White flight from urban areas began to escalate after the 1954 Supreme Court decision in *Brown v. Board of Education*. After efforts were finally stepped up to enforce *Brown* through the desegregation of public schools—almost 15 years later—many White Americans made no secret of their feelings about living near Black people and attending schools with them. They made their feelings clear not only verbally but also by exiting to suburban and outlying communities. In many instances, these actions were facilitated and encouraged by White communities and realtors through race-steering and other means of deterring Black families from moving into predominantly White communities. Urban areas and school systems became less White and increasingly Black.

With the departure of White people from urban schools and communities, the White business elite soon followed and withdrew its support from urban school districts, especially when these cities became predominantly Black and then began to elect Black mayors and predominantly Black school boards.[2] Although African Americans gained some political power in these cities, they still lacked economic resources, which overwhelmingly resided in the hands of Whites. Central city schools became even poorer with the increasing presence of low-income Blacks and the movement of White and some Black middle-class residents away from the city (Massey, 1990; Massey & Eggers, 1990; Quillian, 1999; Wilson, 1987). Therefore, with eroding political and economic bases, urban and predominantly African American communities and schools began to look like concentrated areas of poverty (Jargowsky, 1994; Quillian, 1999; Wilson, 1987).

In addition to the exodus of industries to other countries that began to occur during the 1970s and 1980s, a subsequent decline in manufacturing jobs for low-skilled workers, and the influx of immigrants into low-wage jobs, "invisible" racist practices within the social, political, and the economic structures of U.S. society also limited Black people's opportunities and, therefore, their families' and children's overall life chances (Royster, 2003).[3] Consequently, peddling drugs and other alternative forms of acquiring money became more pervasive in these urban centers. The influx of crack-cocaine into urban areas during the 1980s began to devastate communities that lacked a substantial economic base for poor people who did not have the educational skills essential to gainful employment or the financial resources to leave. The following sections further illustrate how social and historical forces began to shape the contemporary educational situation for low-income African American residents in two cities, St. Louis and Atlanta.

UNDER THE ARCH: THE SCHOOLING OF BLACK FOLKS IN ST. LOUIS

The schooling of African Americans in St. Louis should not be divorced from their history in the city, the racial politics surrounding the question of whether Missouri would enter the Union as a free or slave state, and African Americans' broader experiences in the United States. Missouri entered the Union in 1821 as a slave state. Free and enslaved Africans were among the earliest settlers in the city of St. Louis and the state of Missouri. By the late 1840s, Black people had established schools in the basements of churches throughout the city, including the Chambers Street Baptist Church, First African Methodist Episcopal Church, St. Paul African Methodist Church, and Central Baptist.

However, in 1847, Missouri passed a law that stated: "No person shall keep or teach any school for the instruction of Negroes or mulattos in reading or writing in this STATE" (quoted in Wright, 1994, p. 2). And if caught, there were severe penalties such as a fine and beatings with a whip. This law was passed in response to the abolitionist movement in Missouri and the fear of White slave owners that literate free Blacks would be rebellious.

Despite the imposition of these laws, Black people in St. Louis were still persistent in educating themselves. For example, Reverend John Berry Meachum, a formerly enslaved Black man who became pastor of the First African Baptist Church in St. Louis, built a steamboat and anchored it on the Mississippi River; this steamboat served as a school. Hundreds of Black children were educated in the 1840s and 1850s on this floating school. In 1866, the state of Missouri established the first public schools for Black children in dilapidated rented rooms.

In 1875, African Americans in St. Louis complained to the state legislature about the quality of the educational buildings for their children. Consequently, the Board of Education of St. Louis designated a formerly all-White school to serve as the first high school for "Negroes" in St. Louis. This school was named Sumner High School, in honor of Charles Sumner (1811–1874), a United States Senator who became the first prominent politician to urge the emancipation of enslaved Black people. The end of Reconstruction in the South in 1876 resulted in the return to slavelike conditions for Black people.

During the latter part of the 1870s, the Black population in St. Louis greatly increased when a wave of Black migrants moved west to flee oppressive conditions in the South, where they had "suffered harsh political, social, and economic oppression at the hands of their former slavemasters; these migrants were known as 'Exodusters'" (Wright, 1994, p. 16). Most of the help for these "Exodusters," including food, clothing, and shelter, was provided by Black people who already lived in St. Louis. This kind of communal outreach to Black people from the southern states was crucial in forging a collective Black racial identity in the city.

In 1876, the city of St. Louis annexed a small town known as Elleardsville (the name was shortened to "the 'Ville" and is the area where Fairmont Elementary School is located). The 'Ville was named after Charles Elleards, a horticulturist who built a two-story home and a large nursery in the area. Initially, the community consisted primarily of German and

Irish immigrants. However, some African Americans lived in the community when much of the city was "covered by restrictive real estate covenants which prevented Blacks from owning or renting residential property" (Wright, 1994, p. 75).

Yet White residents of the 'Ville and nearby areas were not particularly welcoming to Black people, who were still regarded as second-class citizens—in practice and by law. For example, on February 16, 1911, even though some Black people had owned property in the area since 1882, 30 out of 39 White property owners signed a covenant barring African American property ownership:

> . . . the said property is hereby restricted to the use and occupancy for the term of Fifty (50) years from this date, so that it shall be a condition all the time and whether recited and referred to as [*sic*] not in subsequent conveyances and shall attach to the land as a condition precedent to the sale of the same, that hereafter no part of said property or any [p. 5] portion thereof shall be, for said term of Fifty-years, occupied by any person not of the Caucasian race, it being intended hereby to restrict the use of said property for said period of time against the occupancy as owners or tenants of any portion of said property for resident or other purpose by people of the Negro or Mongolian Race. (*Shelley v. Kraemer* [1948])

This covenant, however, prompted an important Supreme Court decision that ended restrictive real estate agreements based on race. In *Shelley v. Kraemer* (1948), the Court ruled that the constitutional rights of J.D. Shelley and his family (who were African Americans) had been violated by a 50-year covenant—established by the Marcus Avenue Improvement Association and supported by the Real Estate Board of St. Louis—that barred the sale of houses to persons not of Caucasian descent.

African Americans, despite underemployment, housing and workplace discrimination, inequitable pay, and the relegation to certain types of jobs, still carved out a livelihood for themselves in the 'Ville. Residents of the 'Ville included African Americans who occupied jobs such as teachers, postmen, and factory workers. On St. Louis Avenue, which borders the 'Ville, Black-owned businesses included restaurants, food stores, barbershops, and the offices of dentists, lawyers, and doctors. African Americans from various parts of the city met on St. Louis Avenue. Today, remnants of these businesses remain; old signs on outside walls are reminders of the "Old 'Ville."

During the early part of the 20th century, Black people in St. Louis still developed communities, businesses, and other institutions that served them. In many instances, these businesses and institutions thrived. On the other hand, Black people were not sheltered from the harsh economic and political realities of the day. They were restricted from participating in the broader aspects of St. Louis, legally segregated in schools, and prevented from using public parks and facilities. One well-known example of these restrictions was the 1949 incident at Fairgrounds Park, which borders the 'Ville. The beginnings of a race riot occurred when African American youth were attacked by a group of White youth.

The Fairgrounds Park incident was sparked when the mayor ordered the opening of the city's swimming pools and playgrounds to African Americans. Soon afterwards, approximately 50 Black youths attempted to enter the pool. They were violently attacked by some 200 teenage White youth. After the African American youth were attacked, the mayor rescinded the integration order. One week later, a Council on Human Relations was appointed and voted in April 1950 to gradually open the public swimming pools to African Americans. A minority on the council dissented, favoring an *immediate end* to segregation in all St. Louis recreational facilities. In July 1950, the United States District Court ordered the city of St. Louis to admit Black people to all open-air swimming pools.

In relation to communities and schools, some of the neighborhoods in the northern section of St. Louis quickly became predominantly Black in the 1940s and 1950s. African Americans moved into the area surrounding Fairmont Elementary School, profiled in this book, around 1952. Despite living in the neighborhood, Black children were not allowed to attend the all-White neighborhood elementary school, Fairmont Elementary School. However, Fairmont began to enroll Black students in 1956, two years after the *Brown v. Board of Education* decision. By the late 1960s and early 1970s, the school was transformed into an all-Black school as a result of Black people's influx into the community and White residents' departure.

During the mid-1970s, in *Liddell v. St. Louis Board of Education* (1975, 1979), Black plaintiffs accused the St. Louis Board of Education of contributing to African American children receiving a segregated education in the city's public school system. In 1979, Judge Meredith, who presided over the case, held that there was not adequate evidence to prove that the St. Louis Board of Education had purposefully discriminated against African Americans.

In March 1980, the decision was reversed by the United States Court of Appeals for the Eighth Circuit, which stated that there was adequate evidence of discrimination by the St. Louis Board of Education and the state of Missouri. In July 1980, African American plaintiffs—including community organizations, the NAACP, the city of St. Louis, and a number of the county school systems—approved a voluntary settlement to allow African American students to attend schools in the county school systems. This settlement was reached after the plaintiffs and the St. Louis Board of Education accused the county schools of contributing to the mass exodus to the suburbs of White middle-class families. Dissatisfied with the efforts of the settlement, in 1982 the plaintiffs and the St. Louis Board of Education sued to gain a court-ordered remedy that would establish a metropolitan systemwide school district.

In 1983, to avoid a costly trial, lawyers for the Black plaintiffs, officials from the 23 county districts, and the St. Louis Board of Education entered into a settlement. The county districts participated in this settlement under threat of litigation and the possible loss of control in how their districts would be desegregated. The settlement was comprised of five components: (1) the voluntary desegregation of 16 of the 23 county school districts, (2) the voluntary transfer of White county students to city magnet schools, (3) a quality-of-education package for the all-Black schools in the city, (4) a capital improvement package to restore the deteriorated conditions of the city schools, and (5) the hiring of minority staff in the county school districts.

The settlement specified that the county school districts would accept Black students from the city in order to achieve a 25 percent African American student population. The participating county school districts would receive financial compensation from the state equal to the cost of attendance in the respective county schools. Seven of the 23 county school districts already had an African American student enrollment of at least 25 percent; therefore, they did not have to accept African American transfer students. The transfer plan focused on the remaining 16 districts that enrolled low rates of African American students. The enrollment of African American students in the 16 county districts that participated in the plan ranged from 13 percent to 26 percent.

Since the implementation of the settlement plan in 1983, only 5 of the 16 county districts had reached their planned goal of 25 percent African American student enrollment by the late 1990s. For example, during the 1997–1998 schoolyear, a total of 14,224 students were enrolled in the transfer program between the city and the county school districts. Of these, 12,746 African American students from the city transferred to county schools, whereas 1,478 White students from the 16 participating county districts transferred to magnet schools in St. Louis. As part of the settlement, the court mandated that the magnet schools have at least a 40 percent White student enrollment. During 1997–1998, the racial composition of White students in magnet schools was 46 percent.

By 1999, the state of Missouri and the St. Louis Public School Board had paid almost $2 billion into the plan. The state of Missouri paid $160 million into the desegregation plan during the 1998–1999 academic year.

Approximately $70 million went into funding the St. Louis Public School District's portion of the plan. Examples of enhancements included mandating a maximum student–teacher ratio of 20:1. Sixty million dollars went toward funding the student per-pupil cost for transfer students into the county schools, and the remaining funds paid the city and county transportation costs. By then, the state wanted to end the desegregation plan by declaring that the city district had achieved unitary status—a legal term meaning that the state and the city have done all that is necessary to eliminate the vestiges of legal segregation and will not return to these illegal and discriminatory practices.

On the other hand, lawyers representing the NAACP argued that the transfer plan should continue because of the possible resegregation that would result if the plan ended. A panel of judges, at the request of the state of Missouri, began hearing the court case in March 1996 to establish a deadline for settlement negotiations. The concluding chapter of this book examines the local and national implications of the official ending of voluntary desegregation in St. Louis as well as how the city and surrounding county school systems responded.

BLACK MECCA AND THE DISINHERITED OF ATLANTA

Known as the "city too busy to hate" because of its "skillful" handling of civil unrest and ability to develop interracial alliances, Atlanta offers an interesting paradox when trying to understand the extent to which Black people have made progress in the city and the nation (Sjoquist, 2000). Atlanta's reputation as a "Black Mecca" was solidified by the 1990s, due in part to its increasingly African American population and the perception that the city had unlimited social, political, and economic opportunities for Black people.

Atlanta's designation as a Black Mecca suggests that great progress has occurred, especially considering the fact that during the early and middle part of the 20th century, African Americans left the South en masse—particularly from states like Georgia, Alabama, and Mississippi—because of deep-rooted racism and discrimination, racial violence against Black people, and the lack of educational and economic opportunities. For example, from 1910 to 1920, approximately 525,000 Black people left the South; from 1950 to 1960, more than 1.5 million left the South. In this mass exodus, thousands of Black people headed to the North and Midwest in search of greater social, political, and economic freedoms (Drake & Cayton, 1945; Lemann, 1991).

The modern civil rights movement during the 1950s and 1960s, however, ushered in the beginning of a semblance of more social, economic, and political freedoms for African Americans. In the 1970s and 1980s, the South ceased to be perceived as the bastion of segregation, racism, and discrimination. It became perceived as a place of greater economic opportunities for all ethnic groups, but particularly African Americans, and Atlanta became the economic and social center of the South.

As in other parts of the South and the United States, historically, Black people in Atlanta have endured a tumultuous and enduring quest for quality schooling. During the latter part of the 19th and early 20th centuries (around 1900–1910), the Black struggle for schooling in Atlanta centered largely on the disparity of funding between the White and Black schools. These funding disparities meant that new school buildings were not built and that new teachers were not hired to accommodate the growing Black student population, thus creating overcrowded schooling conditions for African American children. Consequently, many Black children in Atlanta did not attend public schools. Of those who did, many went for only about three hours a day, and these Black schools often held double sessions (Bayor, 1996). During these double sessions, one group of students would attend school during the earlier part of the day; afterwards, another group would attend for the latter part.

African Americans who could afford to sent their children to elementary and high schools offered by the Black colleges in the city. These colleges (Atlanta University, Morris Brown College, Clark College, Spelman College, and Morehouse College) minimized the impact that a racist system of public schooling had on some Black children's education. Although some individuals in the Black community could counter some of the educational disparities with their own institutions, many Black children, particularly those in poverty, suffered educationally.

In addition to providing insufficient schools and classrooms for Black children, in 1913 the all-White Atlanta Board of Education attempted to limit the quality of schooling for Black children by suggesting a plan to eliminate seventh and eighth grades in the Black schools, the two highest grades available in the public schools for Black children. Although this proposal was rejected, when funding issues arose in 1914, Atlanta's Board of Education chose to eliminate eighth grade in the Black schools but allowed White children to have schooling up to the eleventh grade.

In the 1920s, Black people in Atlanta made greater demands on the public school system after the passage of a bond issue that was expected to provide additional funds for the schools. Organizations like the NAACP were very concerned about the conditions of Black education, which consigned Black children to attending schools with double sessions. For example, a 1921–1922 survey by George D. Strayer and N. C. Engelhardt, the Director and Assistant Director, respectively, at Columbia University's Teachers College, to determine how the bond money should be spent reported that while the White schools needed improvement, the Black schools were not fit for children to attend. These Black schools lacked sufficient equipment, playgrounds, and classrooms.[4]

The city of Atlanta did not build its first public junior high school for Black children until 1924. This school, Booker T. Washington High School, was the school that Martin Luther King Jr. would later attend. On the other hand, White children in Atlanta already had eight junior high and senior high schools. Although Black children represented approximately one-third of the population of school-aged children during the 1930s, from the 1930s to the late 1940s, per-pupil expenditure for White students was more than twice that for Black students (Bayor, 1996).

To further underscore the nature of the educational inequalities experienced by Black people, Ms. Murphy, a first-grade teacher at Lincoln Elementary School in Atlanta for 33 years, remembers growing up and experiencing the inequalities of segregation in Atlanta. She attended Booker T. Washington High School during the late 1950s. But Ms. Murphy notes that in the midst of this segregation and inequality, Black educators and schools tried to make sure that Black children were educationally prepared.

> I was at Washington High School [Booker T. Washington High School]. And we achieved. But we had to use reconditioned text books from Roosevelt High School [a White high school]. Now that school is closed. We had reconditioned algebra books from Roosevelt High School, and reconditioned books from Brown High School, which were all-White high schools at that time. I will never forget studying *Julius Caesar* and having to share a desk with another student, and share the book as well, because we had over 3,000 students at Washington High. We had all of these reconditioned books and never really knew what we were given. But yet we learned.

From the 1950s to the 1970s, Atlanta underwent a major demographic shift. Once predominantly White, the city became predominantly Black during the 1970s, partly due to the out-migration of Whites from the city to the suburbs. For example, Mrs. Carr, an African American resident of the Lincoln Elementary community (later highlighted in this book), recounted her experiences when her family moved into the Lincoln community in 1957. Mrs. Carr's statement illustrates how White residents of

Atlanta, in a nondramatic fashion, slowly gave way to the wave of Black migration into parts of the city—particularly the community that surrounded Lincoln Elementary School.

> When we moved here, like I say, it was mostly White and the only thing we really noticed when we moved here, the street was named Lincoln all the way to and from Gale. But as soon as we moved here they changed Lincoln, after you cross, after you cross East Avenue. They changed it to Oak Street. . . . All that happened after the Blacks moved in. 'Cause that's all right, the street is still the street [no matter what happens]. And so I can say one thing about this, the Whites, when we moved in here they were very nice. They didn't bother us and we didn't bother them. But they just steadily moved out.

During the 1960s, initial efforts to desegregate the public schools were resisted by many White public officials and through White citizens' abandonment of public schools. The public school system "officially" became predominantly Black with the inception of what was known as the "Atlanta Compromise" in 1973. Prior to the Atlanta Compromise, the school district went from 32 percent Black in 1952 to 82 percent Black in 1974. In the compromise, lawyers with the local NAACP worked out a plan—supported by some local Black leaders and school board members (including Benjamin E. Mays, a prominent Black educator and former president of Morehouse College)—that called for faculty desegregation and limited pupil desegregation.

Part of the motivation behind this plan was an attempt to stifle "White flight"; to prevent the replacement of Black teachers and principals, which often accompanied efforts to desegregate; and to give voice to African Americans' belief that Black children could achieve in a school system controlled by Black people (Bayor, 1996; Stone, 1989). The compromise also called for the board to hire top Black administrators rather than allow the governance of the district to remain in the hands of White people, who historically had denied equal education to Black children.

Critics argued that the plan created less of a commitment to Atlanta's public schools by the White business and civic elite and produced little educational gain for Black children, particularly those from low-income families (Bayor, 1996; Henig et al., 1999; Orfield & Ashkinaze, 1991). In the late 1970s and 1980s, some middle-class Black families moved into suburbs, and others placed their children in private schools. The public schools in the city overwhelmingly enrolled Black children from families that were poor.

Atlanta's social, political, and economic blossoming above the rest of the South during the 1980s and 1990s did little to address a significant population of its citizens—the Black underclass. This group became the "dis-inheritors" of the civil rights movement, a movement that was sometimes inattentive to the inextricable link between race and social class. Consequently, in the middle of a seeming oasis of opportunity for Black people, more than one-third of Atlanta's families lived below the poverty line (U.S. Census Bureau, 2000).[5]

From 2000 to 2004, the percentage of children in Atlanta living in poverty increased from 39.3 percent to 48.1 percent, thus making Atlanta the *number-one-ranked city in the United States in terms of percentage of children living in poverty* (U.S. Census Bureau, 2004a). This is a serious commentary on the "city too busy to hate" and the "Black Mecca." As the city continued its economic upward mobility during the 1990s and early 2000s, the struggle for quality education, particularly for those who are poor and Black, continues to be a major paradox.

This historical synopsis of Black schooling in the two urban centers profiled in this book illustrates how a historical legacy of racism, discrimination, and poverty contributed to contemporary schooling conditions for African American people in these and other urban centers of the United States. Throughout this history, discriminatory policies in the broader society and the schooling structure—over extended periods of time—set in motion the adverse social and economic conditions that many poor Black people are faced with today. As illustrated throughout this book, these conditions have resulted in blighted communities inhabited disproportionately by Black people at the bottom of America's social and economic structure. This is the social, economic, and schooling reality for millions of African American children today.

PART II

Beyond Central Cities: In Search of *Brown's* Second Promise

CHAPTER 3

Whosoever Will, Can They Come?
Black Families and Choices
in a Magnet School

While they have been overshadowed by recent policy discussions around school choice such as vouchers and charter schools, magnet schools continue to be quietly used as desegregation tools and as a form of school choice, thereby shaping the nature and character of urban schooling today. To encourage White parents to participate in desegregation efforts, many urban school systems in the 1970s and 1980s created magnet schools in response to the mandate of public school desegregation. In 1976, incentives to motivate the voluntary transfer of students were approved by two federal courts in *Arthur v. Nyquist* (1976) in Buffalo, New York, and *Amos v. Board of Directors of the City of Milwaukee* (1976). In these decisions, the courts relied on magnet schools to desegregate predominantly Black schools and used majority-to-minority transfers to desegregate predominantly White schools.

The late 1970s and early 1980s witnessed the emergence of magnet schools as a major mechanism to aid in the desegregation of public schools. Magnet schools have been introduced into more urban school districts as a means of achieving racial balance in schools and of promoting greater choices in the attempt to satisfy parents' interests and priorities (Smrekar & Goldring, 1999). More than one-half of all large urban school districts have included magnet programs to promote public school desegregation.

In response to the mandate of school desegregation issued by *Brown*, magnet schools used various curricular themes to attract students from ethnically segregated neighborhoods. Rather than "forcing" students to attend desegregated schools, magnet schools ensured diversity with the requirement that the schools reflect some degree of racial balance, usually a ratio of 50 percent White to 50 percent minority. However, critics of magnet schools argued that these schools usually enrolled a disproportionate number of White students because of selection criteria, which favored White students in order to ensure racial balance in these urban schools

(Moore & Davenport, 1989). Amid the promises of magnet schools regarding equitable schooling, these schools do not erase some of the inequitable schooling experiences that Black students face. For example, the gap between disciplinary actions imposed on Black students and on White students is greater in magnet schools in comparison to regular public schools (Morris & Goldring, 1999).

In general, there is a lot of misunderstanding among the public about magnet schools' roles in creating desegregated schools and in promoting school choice. Magnet schools fulfill two purposes: In theory, these schools (1) advance the civil rights cause by creating racially desegregated schools while at the same time (2) providing school choices for parents who want to expand the educational options for their children. In essence, magnet schools further assured White parents that their choice to send their children to public schools in central cities would not compromise the quality of their children's schooling.

Moreover, the mention of magnet schools connotes to many Black parents the image of high-quality schooling—the kind that one does not expect to find in regular public schools (Morris & Fuller, 2007).[1] So it is no surprise that Black parents clamor for their children to attend these schools. For many, just getting their children into magnet schools represents the fulfillment of *Brown*'s promise of quality schooling. But why do some Black parents choose to send their children to magnet schools while others do not? Is there a social-class element involved in knowing about the various choices? Of the parents who choose magnet schools, what sources inform them about the opportunities that these schools afford? Moreover, once their children are enrolled in these schools, what kinds of relationships do school personnel forge with Black parents and their children? Such relationships are critical for ensuring the educational success of Black children in schools that are predicated on providing educational excellence and diversity. Ethnographic insights from Denson Magnet School in St. Louis provide some clues to this litany of questions.

INSIDE DENSON MAGNET SCHOOL

Built in 1917, Denson Magnet School is nestled on the outskirts of St. Louis near the Clayton School District. The school is located in a primarily working to middle-class and predominantly White residential community. The school campus encompasses almost an entire city block. Well-kept flowerbeds line the front walkway leading up to the school. A sign posted on the school gate reads, "Do not walk dogs on school grounds." Two entrances lead up to the school; one was closed off. To enter the school building, one has to ring the doorbell to be buzzed in by Ms. Crest, the secretary.

Inside the building, the thematic focus of the school is evident: Denson is an international studies magnet school. The foyer resembles the kind of corridor that one might imagine would be inside the United Nations building. The area is elaborately adorned with flags from around the world. A quilt with patches in the shape of different countries hangs on the wall outside the main office. School paraphernalia also convey an international theme. During the mid-1990s, *Redbook* magazine selected Denson as "the best school in the state" of Missouri. Students are required to take at least two foreign languages, choosing from Russian, German, French, and Spanish. Assemblies and programs emphasize Denson's thematic focus by highlighting various cultures and countries around the world.

Throughout the school, classroom doors are covered with posters and students' work depicting European, Asian, African, and North and South American countries, some of which are adopted by each classroom. African maps, masks, and posters adorn the doors of two classrooms on the second floor. The teachers in these two classrooms adopt African countries to study during the year; both are African American. One of these teachers, Mrs. Collins, won the "Teacher of the Year" award in Missouri and represented the St. Louis public school system in Washington, D.C.

Whereas Denson Magnet School used to be surrounded by White families whose children once attended the school, White senior citizens now make up the majority of the residents in the neighborhood. Today, very few students come from the neighborhood; instead, they come from neighborhoods all over the city. One of these neighborhoods is the 'Ville in the northern part of St. Louis. Most of the parents from the 'Ville send their children to the neighborhood elementary school, Fairmont, but a few choose to send their children to Denson. Given the options afforded to African American parents as part of the desegregation plan, why did some African American parents decide to participate in the desegregation plan and send their children to schools outside their neighborhood?

Although a neighborhood elementary school for decades, Denson became a magnet school in 1989 and was one of 26 magnet schools in the city of St. Louis that had to adhere to mandates from the desegregation court order, which required that magnet schools enroll a racially diverse population of students. Admission to the school was governed by the magnet school enrollment policies established in the desegregation court order, which allowed any student who lived in St. Louis, and any White student who lived in the participating suburban school districts, the option of attending the St. Louis public school system's magnet schools. The admission process involved a lottery. Applications were accepted from the beginning of December until the end of February of the upcoming academic year. Seats were generally filled by the middle of March.

First priority for magnet enrollment was given to promote educational continuity and to allow siblings to attend the same school together. For example, if a student (Black or White) was currently enrolled in a magnet school and wished to continue on to another school with the same theme, priority was given to that student. Second priority was provided to students (Black or White) living at the same address who applied to a sibling's magnet school. For Black students, third priority was given to students in the city who attended the "nonintegrated" (predominantly Black) schools in the city. Fourth priority for Black students was given to those residing in the city, regardless of the status of the school they attended. For example, some of the Black and White students attended schools that were considered "naturally integrated" due to racially balanced neighborhood attendance zones. Students enrolled in these schools, however, received the lowest priority for magnet school consideration.

For White students who wanted to attend the St. Louis public school system's magnet schools, third priority was given to eligible county students from participating suburban school districts that had low rates of White students participating in the transfer plan. Fourth priority was given to all other White students living in the city, regardless of the status of the school they attended. The Voluntary Interdistrict Coordinating Council (VICC), which was created during the settlement negotiations and approved by the court, coordinated the transfer of White students from the county into magnet schools.[2]

Denson Magnet School enrolled students from just about every neighborhood in the city of St. Louis, including White students from the participating suburban school districts. Daily, 27 buses picked up and dropped off children. Enrollment at the school was approximately 450 students (prekindergarten through fifth grade), with a racial breakdown of 55 percent African American students, 35 percent White students, and 10 percent international students (which included English as a Second Language). Sixty-three percent of the students received free or reduced lunches, which allowed the school to receive Title I funds. These federal funds provided schools with a significant number of low-income students, additional resources for professional development, instructional support, educational programs, and parent involvement.[3]

The faculty and staff makeup at Denson was about one-fourth African American and three-fourths White. There were 19 classroom teachers; of these teachers, four were African American and 15 were White. The four language teachers (Russian, French, Spanish, and German) were White; these four teachers also had two African American assistants working with them. The principal and the instructional coordinator were both African American females.

Of the seven African American families from the 'Ville whose children attended Denson, three had connections with the school system, either as teacher assistants or as a retired teacher (see Table 3.1). Furthermore, a parent from only one of the seven families had not finished high school. Three of the families had a parent who had completed or attended college, and three had a parent who had finished high school. Although

Table 3.1. Denson family profiles, selected African American students.

FAMILY	COMMUNITY AFFILIATION	OCCUPATION	EDUCATION	YEARS IN COMMUNITY
King: Grandparents; daughter and two grandchildren	Their children attended Fairmont.	Mrs. King: Retired teacher Mr. King: Retired mechanic	Mrs. King: BS Mr. King: High school diploma	40
Carson: Married parents; three children	Mrs. Carson: worked as a teaching assistant at Fairmont during summer school.	Mrs. Carson: Teaching assistant Mr. Carson: Drafting technician	Mrs. Carson: Three years of college Mr. Carson: Attended community college	12
Clark: Single mother; three children	None.	Unemployed; receives AFDC (TANF)	Completed high school	2
Dwight: Married parents; four children	Mrs. Dwight attended Fairmont.	Mrs. Dwight: Former teaching assistant, currently secretary Mr. Dwight: Postal clerk	Mrs. Dwight: BS Mr. Dwight: High school diploma	Both parents grew up in community
Henson: Single mother; one child	Attended Fairmont.	Cashier	Completed tenth grade	3
Pearson: Divorced mother; three children	Attended Fairmont.	Unemployed	Completed high school	Moved out of the community and later returned
Winston: Divorced, mother; four children	None.	Factory	Completed high school	Moved into mother's house in the community for two years

these social-class indicators do not drastically differ from those of the parents whose children attended the predominantly African American neighborhood elementary school, Fairmont, they are, nevertheless, slightly higher, providing some credence to the role of social class in influencing who gets access to quality schooling.[4]

CHOOSING DENSON: AFRICAN AMERICAN PARENTS' REASONS

Why did some of the African American families from the 'Ville choose to send their children to Denson Magnet School instead of the predominantly African American neighborhood elementary school to which their children were assigned? What role did social class play in this process? There were similarities among many of these African American parents, particularly their access to informational networks, which academics and scholars term "social capital." In general, social capital theory focuses on the benefits accruing to individuals as a result of their ties to others.[5] Some of the Black parents whose children attended Denson were privy to information that placed them in a better position to choose, in comparison to most of the Black parents in the city.

Although these parents did not work in high-status occupations and were not from what social scientists would define as middle-class backgrounds, they nevertheless possessed a greater degree of informational networks than did other Black parents from the community. For example, two of the parents were teaching assistants and another—a grandparent— was a retired teacher.[6] As one parent said, "I knew [more] about any information concerning magnet schools than most parents, because I worked in a magnet school." Another mother, Mrs. Carson, who had previously worked in the schools and understood the application process involved in selecting students, explained to me how she worked to ensure that her children were enrolled in the magnet school of her choice:

> With my first daughter, I was not totally sure that she would be picked in the lottery for the magnet school. I signed her up when she was 4 years old. Since then, I decided to put my name on the magnet waiting list when my youngest daughter was 2 years old. Since she had two sisters already in the magnet school, it was going to be much easier for my last daughter to go to Denson.

As an African American parent whose children attended St. Louis public schools, Mrs. Carson knew that she had to be very proactive in getting her children into one of the few coveted magnet school spots in the district. Consequently, she signed her child up for magnet schools at the age of 2 in order to increase her chances of being selected to attend a magnet school. As is the policy in many magnet school programs, priority would be given to students with siblings who already attended magnet schools—thereby making it much easier for subsequent children to be admitted to the school. Mrs. Carson understood and articulated this. Her point also has to be understood within the context of the sense of urgency among some African American parents to ensure quality education for their children, knowing the limited available spaces for them in magnet schools. Unfortunately, the competition for scarce spaces in magnet schools in urban centers meant that some Black children would be selected while many others would not.

Some of the African American parents' reasons for choosing Denson were connected to their desire for a special curriculum or the accelerated academic environment that magnet schools could provide. For instance, Ms. Pearson, a parent who already had two children in the neighborhood African American elementary school, decided to enroll a third child in Denson. The major reason she chose Denson for this third child was because of her daughter's "academic abilities" and interest in international study. Interest in the international studies and language component of the school was also echoed by Ms. Henson, another parent who said that she wanted her daughter "to learn a foreign language. She [her daughter] said she wanted to do some work with people from different countries."

While particular children's ability levels and special interests prompted some parents to send their children to Denson, others chose for different reasons. For example, Ms. Winston, a parent who had recently moved into the 'Ville during the time of the study, said that she chose Denson as an alternative to the neighborhood school because "It was going to be either the magnet school or I would enroll my children in county schools." Ms. Winston did not feel that the public schools in St. Louis, particularly on the northern and predominantly African American side of the city, could adequately prepare her child. Consequently, she sought a school beyond the neighborhood.

Unlike the other parents, Ms. Winston did not grow up in the community or have a previous affiliation with the neighborhood elementary school. A common pattern emerged while inquiring into why some of these parents chose particular schools: Parents who once attended Fairmont Elementary School or grew up in the community were more likely to consider Fairmont—the neighborhood elementary school—to be a "very good school" because of its academic reputation and enduring connection with families from the neighborhood. Consider the following response by

Ms. Pearson, who once attended the neighborhood school and who had moved in and out of the community on several occasions:

> I would say that Fairmont has a lot more opportunities than the other grade schools. I was always pleased with Fairmont. My oldest son went there from second grade to fifth grade. My oldest daughter went there from pre-school to fifth grade.

Ms. Pearson's comment was indicative of the nuanced reasons why parents made certain choices, particularly in relation to the neighborhood school. When given a quality predominantly Black school as one of their choices, these parents overwhelmingly chose the school. For example, only ten families from the entire community chose for their children to attend schools other than the predominantly Black elementary school that their children were zoned to attend; seven families chose Denson Magnet School and three families chose a predominantly White suburban school, which is profiled in Chapter 6.

Although Black parents were very comfortable with sending their children to the neighborhood elementary school, they were very reluctant to send these same children to the neighborhood middle school—Thomas Middle School. For the most part, these parents did not view Thomas Middle School as a safe and academically sound school. Consequently, the parents began to look to middle schools outside their neighborhood. When asked what middle school their child would attend, parents who had children enrolled in the neighborhood elementary school offered the following responses:

> Right now, we are looking into some of the magnet school programs that are offered in the city, and Dampier School is one of them. Hopefully, he will be chosen for one of the magnet schools. (Mrs. Greene, a neighborhood school parent)

> I don't really want my son to go there to the middle school that Fairmont sends most of its kids to [Thomas Middle School]. . . . Also, the neighborhood up there is pretty rough. It cuts right through an area of the neighborhood that I would not feel comfortable with him walking through. (Ms. Roseman, a neighborhood school parent)

African American parents' assessment of Thomas Middle School was not unfounded. The school's location and physical presence were not inviting. Its architecture lacked the grandeur of a Fairmont, and the school had developed a reputation for having an unstable staff and administrative unit. The school was eventually closed as a result of the school district's shrinking student population.

The fact that these African American parents did not want their children to attend the neighborhood middle school cannot be overlooked. These parents' descriptions of the middle school conjure up images of neglected inner-city schools that are pervasive in scholarly literature and in the minds of the lay public. And, in many ways, one cannot blame Black parents, particularly low-income ones who reside in U.S. urban centers, for desiring schools that better serve their children. For example, African American parents are some of the most ardent supporters of school choice—even though school choice is often advocated by conservatives and is also deemed by liberals not to be in the overall interest of low-income Black children.

However, scholars and policy makers have to think more deeply about why low-income African American parents embrace some aspects of public school choice. Unlike middle-class parents (Black or White) who can exercise educational options by choosing to live in certain neighborhoods where the public schools are considered good, by sending their children to private schools, or by home-schooling their children, poor Black parents just do not have these housing and educational options; thus, they are left to take whichever schools are given to them—be they good or bad. Therefore, magnet schools, as these parents attest, become the best public school option, particularly at the middle school level.

Yet magnet schools have limitations in terms of the number of children who will get selected. And magnet schools do not necessarily ensure equitable schooling for Black children, particularly if such schools do not have school leaders who will advocate on behalf of African American children. For example, a study of the disciplinary rates of Black and White students in magnet schools found that magnet schools were similar to traditional public schools in their rate of disciplining Black students (Morris & Goldring, 1999). The enrollment of African American students in magnet schools does not guarantee the equitable treatment of the children in those schools. As the following attests, certain factors within magnet schools constrain opportunities for Black families' presence.

OPPORTUNITIES AND CONSTRAINTS
FOR BLACK PARENTS' PRESENCE

Despite publicity efforts by the administrators at Denson Magnet School to involve parents in the school, Mrs. Woodson—the African American principal at Denson—believed that "Denson is not where it should be as far as involving the African American parents." Opportunities for parental participation at Denson began with the parent–teacher organization (PTO), which played a vital link in cultivating relations among parents, teachers, and the school. The PTO organized fund-raisers and sponsored such activities as yard sales, tailgate sales, and parent–teacher luncheons. There were eleven parent officers in the PTO; nine were White and two were African American.

Throughout the schoolyear, parents could be seen at the school assisting teachers, serving as chaperones on field trips, or attending assemblies. A luncheon sponsored by the PTO was indicative of the very minor Black parent presence in the school. Of the more than twenty parents in attendance at this luncheon, only four were Black. The PTO president, a White female, expressed the difficulty she experienced trying to get some of the African American parents to attend PTO meetings and other events:

> We usually have pretty good involvement from some of our parents. Some of the parents can't come up to the meetings because they don't have transportation. See, our parents live everywhere. Our African American parents come from all over.

Time constraints, busy work schedules, and the lack of transportation impacted some of the African American parents' abilities to participate at Denson. This was more evident among the single African American parents, such as the following mother: "I work a third shift at a service station; I am tired in the morning when I come home from work. I don't get up until about noon." Another African American parent attributed her lack of presence and involvement in the school to the unavailability of transportation:

> I can't make it up to the school as much as I would like because my car works whenever it wants to work. I have to take my 2-year-old daughter with me on the bus, too. I don't care too much for having to catch the bus up to the school.[7]

The instructional coordinator, Mrs. Bethune (who is African American), echoed how work schedules and other time constraints were major obstacles to some African American parents' participation:

> I think that one of the problems that we have, specifically for our African American parents, is that they sometimes are not able to make it up to the school. Our Black parents work. I'm not saying

that our White parents don't work, but almost all of our Black parents work. Also, many of the African American parents don't have transportation up to the school.

In addition to time constraints and work schedules, Mrs. Woodson also believed that some of the African American parents were not as involved in the school because they perceived schools to be intimidating and unwelcoming places:

> I think those parents that are disillusioned by the system are those who might have felt uncomfortable and may have had negative experiences in the school. Many times parents have thrown their hands up.

The general public is quick to conclude that if a parent does not participate regularly in the affairs of the school, then that parent does not value her or his child's schooling or may not be involved in other ways. Rather than embrace this way of thinking, Mrs. Woodson believed that schools should be more assertive in involving African American parents— particularly those who are low-income—in their children's school. Mrs. Woodson describes how she has encouraged African American parents to play a greater role in the school:

> I notice that the Black parents want to help their children, but in many instances, they do not know how. I try to let the parents know that they can be involved in their children's education. I try to show them the little things they can do.

Some parents heeded Mrs. Woodson's encouragement. Despite rarely visiting her children's schools due to her job schedule, Ms. Henson talked about taking her children on field trips in the city:

> I take my children to the St. Louis Science Center, the museums, and the zoo. There are other children in my neighborhood that I take with me. We pack up in my car and we all head down to the zoo, the museum, or whatever.

The popular rhetoric regarding Black children's academic disparities has greatly emphasized the role that Black parents play in undermining their children's academic achievement. From scholars such as the late John Ogbu (2003), to the husband-and-wife team of Abigail and Stephan Thernstrom (2003), and to famous comedians such as Bill Cosby, Black parents have been blamed as the primary reason for their children's academic failure in school—rather than the social forces that limit the extent to which families, particularly those who are low-income, can make informed decisions and actively participate in the affairs of the school. Schools also play a critical role in cultivating a welcoming ethos for parents, thereby minimizing obstacles to parents' involvement in the school.

EDUCATORS AND BLACK PARENTS' RELATIONSHIPS

As a racially desegregated school, how could Denson forge meaningful relationships with African American families even though these families were from communities that were many miles from the school? While the PTO functioned as the formal organization for parents to participate at Denson, only a few African American parents regularly attended these meetings. Mrs. Woodson and Mrs. Bethune, the principal and instructional coordinator, respectively, also attributed Black parents' low presence in the school to the school's history as an elite and predominantly White school:

> At one time, Denson Magnet School had a reputation for being a somewhat elite school. Many of the Black parents did not participate in the school. The PTO would be mainly all White. We have tried to change that some. We now try to make sure the Black parents know what's going on up here at the school. We have two Black parents on the PTO this year. (Mrs. Bethune)

Not only did the African American educational leaders at Denson work to involve African American parents in the school, they also assisted in resolving cultural misunderstandings and other conflicts that emerged between African American parents and teachers:

> A teacher, who was White, asked me if I could come up to the school to talk about my child, and she asked if I worked. I didn't appreciate her asking me a question like that. I went off on the teacher when she asked me if I worked. (Ms. Winston)

Ms. Winston eventually went to the school to speak with the teacher. She said, "Mrs. Woodson [the principal] came looking for me because she thought that I might jump on the teacher. I told the teacher, 'Don't you talk to me like that again because I was about to whoop your butt!'" Ms. Winston, who was recently divorced, was gainfully employed. However, whether correctly or incorrectly, she appears to have interpreted the teacher's statement as a judgment—one that is rooted in pervasive perceptions of Black women in the United States as loud, angry, and welfare dependents (Hill-Collins, 2000, 2004).[8]

The best description of Black parents' relationships with educators at Denson is that it was enigmatic in nature. For example, Denson offered foreign language courses to students and parents who were not proficient in English. The faculty and staff also agreed to rearrange International Day to accommodate parents who worked second-shift jobs. Rather than schedule the program in the evening, the school held the celebration from the beginning of the schoolday until the early evening. Mrs. Woodson explained the change:

> Some of the parents from different countries, and particularly Black parents, worked second and third shifts. Consequently, we decided it was best that the International Day was held throughout the schoolday. That way, they could come up to the school when they had time available.

Ms. Clark, a Black parent, described how some of the teachers at the school supported her and her family:

> They were real supportive one year and had a fund-raiser to help my children at Mathews Dickey [a local boys' club] to go to Atlanta. I had a fish fry and everything to raise money for my children to go to Atlanta, Georgia. The Black teachers in the school helped out by buying fish dinners.

Ms. Winston further noted how the administrators supported her by understanding the difficulty that she was experiencing as a result of her recent divorce:

> The school [administration] was very understanding, at times, about my situation as a divorced parent. I have had to express issues to people about the fact that my children might be acting a certain way because of me going through a divorce.

Ms. Henson, a single African American parent, also described the supportive nature of the school and how Denson's administrators and faculty understood the reasons for her daughter's chronic tardiness, which she attributed to her own hectic work schedule:

The school has put up with me. Instead of punishing her [my daughter] for me bringing her to school late, they excused her being tardy. At another school when my daughter was real late, they called social services on me. I told them that I wasn't on drugs but that I worked until two in the morning and be tired when I take her to school in the mornings. I don't have to worry about that now because she gets ready by herself in the morning.

Denson supported families' unique situations and experiences by offering English courses to foreign-born parents and their children, by accommodating parents' schedules to enable them to participate at the school, and by allowing flexibility in school policies. However, the support for the Black parents came primarily from the African American administrators: the principal and the instructional coordinator, Mrs. Woodson and Mrs. Bethune, respectively.

SCHOOL LEADERS AS ADVOCATES IN RACIALLY DIVERSE SCHOOLS

Mrs. Woodson, the principal, was known at Denson as an ardent advocate for the children. Prior to her tenure at Denson, Mrs. Woodson was the principal of an all-Black neighborhood school with an Afrocentric thematic focus—a perspective that focused heavily on educating African American children from the strengths of their cultural perspective (Asante, 1987; Hilliard, 2003). Mrs. Woodson was adamant that the school's curriculum recognize the culture and historical heritage of African American students. After serving as the principal at the Afrocentric thematic school for 4 years, Mrs. Woodson was reassigned to Denson because of her reputation as an advocate for Black children. As she said:

Here at Denson, we have to be advocates for Black children because we can't divorce ourselves from who we are. I can't separate my roles as parent, teacher, and particularly Black parent, from myself as a principal in St. Louis public schools.

According to many of the teachers at the school, prior to Mrs. Woodson's tenure, Denson did little to involve the African American children and parents in the affairs of the school. However, the Director of Elementary Schools, who was African American, was confident that Mrs. Woodson could help the Black students have a more equitable educational experiences and that African American families could play a more active role in the school. According to Mrs. Bethune, "The director chose her [Mrs. Woodson] because she was committed to Black children. He followed her career and chose her because of her strength and the confidence he had in her abilities."

Immediately upon assuming her duties as principal, Mrs. Woodson focused on promoting equitable educational opportunities for Black students. She took the initiative to include more Black students in the gifted program. She was aware that throughout the public schools in the United States, Black students were often underrepresented in programs for gifted children (Ford & Harris, 1999; Morris, 2002) and disproportionately placed in lower academic tracks (Lucas, 1999; Lucas & Berends, 2007; Oakes, 1985). Mrs. Woodson was intent on changing the underrepresentation of the African American students in the gifted education program:

> We can't blame the children; we have to blame the adults. I am not going to have these children failing. When they have a disproportionate number of White students in gifted as opposed to Black, I said "Well, we'll have a pilot program." Now we have more African American children in the gifted program than before.

Mrs. Woodson's efforts to create an equitable educational environment at Denson for the African American students reflected a genuine concern to enhance the educational opportunities for African American children and were illustrative of characteristics described as qualities of effective administrators for Black children (Lomotey, 1989). Mrs. Bethune, the instructional coordinator, provided most of the support for and rapport with the Black parents at Denson, and she cultivated the relations among parents, teachers, and students. As one parent said, "She is the glue that keeps the school together." Another parent called Mrs. Bethune "an angel." "She does whatever she can to help teachers and parents. She knows every child's name that attends Denson."

Mrs. Bethune would often leave her office to walk through the school building to greet children, welcome parents, or eat lunch with teachers. She was very supportive of parents but especially focused her energy on reaching out to parents who did not regularly attend PTO meetings or frequent the school. According to Mrs. Bethune, "The school needs to do whatever it can to involve the African American parents who are not participating at the school." Mrs. Bethune complimented Mrs. Woodson's very straightforward leadership style by serving as a staunch supporter of all parents (especially African American), teachers, and students.

VALIDATING AND IGNORING RACE
AND CULTURE AT DENSON

Cultural difference theorists such as Jacqueline Jordan Irvine (1990), Gloria Ladson-Billings (1994), and Lisa Delpit (1995) have described how White teachers, who comprise almost 90 percent of the public school teaching force in the United States, often ignore the impact of race and culture in their classrooms. Vivian Paley (1989), in *White Teacher*, discussed how she, a White teacher, would often ignore the dynamics of race when she taught African American children.

There was a general assumption among educators at Denson that they recognized and built on children's diverse cultural experiences, in part because the school was an international studies magnet school. Although Denson's student population was racially diverse, most of the classroom teachers were White females. Additionally, like most U.S. schools with a foreign language focus the languages offered in the school included French, Russian, German, and Spanish. Although this was an international studies magnet school, no African or Asian language was part of the school's focus.[9]

In the interviews with the African American teachers, teaching assistants, and administrators, there were repeated comments that the White teachers at Denson were not as inclusive of the African American students' cultural experiences as these African American educators would have liked them to have been. Mrs. Collins, an African American teacher, said, "I make sure that my children are studying an African country each year. If I didn't, I don't think the other [White] teachers would do it." Other proactive measures were taken by Black faculty to recognize Black students' cultural heritages. For example, Mrs. Woodson informed the faculty and staff of the dietary constraints for the Muslim students and their custom of fasting during the month of Ramadan.[10]

As a former principal of a school with an Afrocentric theme, Mrs. Woodson consciously took steps to ensure that African American students' cultural heritage was validated in the school. School assemblies recognized Dr. King's Birthday and Black History Month. During the December holiday season, there was a concerted effort by the school administrators to recognize holiday celebrations from various cultures and countries; Hanukkah and Kwanzaa were two of the holidays recognized and celebrated. There were also programs and assemblies that featured an array of cultures and countries.

Although Denson openly displayed acceptance of the cultural heritages of its students, school personnel struggled when they had to engage deeper issues of race and culture, beyond the heroes and holidays approach to celebrating culture.[11] Similarly, throughout the United States, schools and educators in public schools often avoid serious analyses of race and racism in schools and society, and many educators have not critically examined their relative positions within personal and global contexts. And when educators do attempt to be more multicultural, the focus for many of them is primarily on heroes, holidays, ethnic foods, and cultural attire—devoid of serious analyses of race- and class-based inequities.

For example, Mrs. Ewen, a White teacher at Denson, stated that she did not see the race of the children: "I only see children. It does not matter to me what race they are. I don't care if they are Black, White, or polka dot." Ladson-Billings (1994) noted that statements such as the one made by Mrs. Ewen are ways that White teachers often trivialize the role that race plays in American society. Mrs. King, an African American grandparent of a child at Denson and also a retired teacher after 40 years in the St. Louis public school system, further illustrated how some White teachers in St. Louis and nationwide ignore the experiences that African American children bring into schools:

> I have taught for many years and I know that many White teachers are not familiar with the experiences of Black children. One of the problems in St. Louis public schools is that the White teachers don't know how to work with Black children. Many of these teachers now don't know anything about the children and don't care. They just come to work and then go home.

One example of this cultural incongruence involved the appropriate strategies that teachers should use to discipline the African American children in the school. One parent said that she was having problems with her child's preschool teacher because of the teacher's disciplinary style. The teacher often called her about the behavior of her 4-year-old son. The parent, Ms. Clark, told the teacher, "You need to put some bass in your voice. If you let a little 4-year-old run over you, then you need to be run over." Ms. Clark commented that the teacher's aide, who was an African American female, "works well with the Black children. The Black teaching assistant understood the difference in how to discipline the Black children. She never had any problems."

It is simple to say that the solution to the above situation is to hire more African American teachers to teach the African American students at Denson. However, the hiring of additional Black teachers would not necessarily ensure that these and other issues would be mitigated. The evidence on the effects of matching Black teachers with Black students is mixed (Alexander, Entwisle, & Thompson, 1987; Dee, 2001), and teachers' social-class background can be just as important as race (Ferguson,

1998a, 1998b). For example, Alexander and colleagues (1987) analyzed data from 20 Baltimore schools and concluded that "the best results for Black students, especially in mathematics, were associated with Black teachers of low socioeconomic status and White teachers of high socio-economic status" (p. 349). Thus, it is possible that an African American teacher can make a difference for Black children—but more so if that particular African American teacher understands and identifies with the social-class experiences of the children that he or she teaches.

But even if Mrs. Woodson wanted to hire more Black teachers at Denson, she was constrained by the district's selection process:

> The central office sent me three White teachers to select from, rather than me having some input in who came out here for an interview. What ended up happening is that we eventually had to choose from the three White teachers they sent. Is that really a choice? I was not involved in selecting the original pool of applicants from which to choose.

While Mrs. Woodson wanted to increase the percentage of African American teachers at the school, the school was already experiencing tensions between the existing White and Black faculty members. These tensions appeared to have emerged once the Black teacher presence in the school became more prominent. Not only did the percentage of African American teachers increase in the school, but also the school's leadership became predominantly African American. The racial dynamics among the staff and faculty would have implications for the schooling experiences of African American students in this racially diverse school.

WHY ARE ALL OF THE WHITE TEACHERS
ON THE FIRST FLOOR?

Diversity scholars often highlight the interracial friendships and relations that are forged by attending and working in racially desegregated contexts. Students who have attended desegregated schools are often more comfortable around students from different backgrounds than students who have not (Tatum, 1997; Wells, Holmes, Atanda, & Revilla, 2005). In terms of the relationships developed among educators in magnet schools, some researchers have described a greater sense of collegiality (McNeil, 1987; Metz, 1986; Raywid, 1989; Smrekar & Goldring, 1999). The basis for this collegiality is what is known as a "value community" created among those teachers who chose to teach in magnet schools.

Although Denson's student and teacher populations were racially diverse, the faculty and staff were ideologically and physically divided along racial lines. These divisions cut across both professional and personal aspects of their lives. For example, almost every day a group of Black teachers regularly went out to lunch together or ate lunch together in Mrs. Collins's room. In contrast, the White teachers typically ate their lunches in the teachers' lounge or in a teacher's classroom. This separation was widely known to parents and other guests who frequented the school. Mrs. Carson, an African American parent, remarked: "I walked into a classroom at the end of the year and saw all of the White teachers talking and enjoying themselves in there. Now, I was not bothered by this, I just spoke to them."

It is not enough to ask, "Why are all of the Black kids sitting together in the cafeteria?" (Tatum, 1997). White and Black school personnel in this racially diverse school, and many others, also operated in similar racially stratified ways. Race played a significant role in shaping the relationships between the White and African American faculty and staff at Denson. Just because it was a magnet school that was created as part of the desegregation plan did not mean that the school would automatically have meaningful relationships between teachers across racial lines. In desegregation plans throughout the United States, an overlooked aspect has been the desegregation of the faculty and the staff. The racial composition of the faculty and staff at Denson was determined by mandates governing the desegregation plan.

Most of the White teachers at Denson, with the exception of some teachers like Mr. Mark (a White kindergarten teacher), were reluctant to discuss the transfer plan or issues regarding race and diversity within the school. Tensions around the St. Louis desegregation plan made many of the White educators reluctant to openly discuss issues of race. People throughout the city of St. Louis, teachers included, had strong opinions.

During the interview for the research study on the desegregation plan, Mr. Mark, mentioned above, wore an earring and a T-shirt with the famous picture of Malcolm X and Dr. Martin Luther King Jr. shaking hands. Mr. Mark was born and raised in St. Louis, attended its public schools, and had been a teacher for 20 years in the St. Louis public school system. In contrast to Mr. Mark, two White teachers at Denson declined to be interviewed. Initially, one of them agreed to be interviewed, but she did not show up and later said she had forgotten about it. The interview was rescheduled, but, upon reading the consent letter, this teacher declined to participate by saying, "Maybe you should talk to someone else." Another teacher said that she was "not the best person to interview. Maybe you should get someone else."[12]

On the other hand, the African American teachers and staff members were enthusiastic in voicing their views about the desegregation plan. This was evident in informal conversations with African American personnel in the school such as Mr. James, the head custodian:

> The [transfer part of] the deseg [desegregation] plan messes up Black children by taking them out of their communities and sending them into the White county schools where they don't care about Black children! I am not for the deseg plan!

The organization of the school building by classrooms also magnified the perception of a separation between White and Black teachers at Denson. The first floor consisted primarily of White teachers' classrooms (all but three of the African American faculty or staff members had their classrooms on the second floor). Ms. Mims, an African American teacher, described the school:

> The White teachers are on the first floor, and the Black teachers are on the second floor. We told Ms. Jones [an African American fifth-grade teacher at the school] that she is the only Black classroom teacher down there with those folks.

The administrators—Mrs. Woodson and Mrs. Bethune—were aware of and said they were very concerned with the appearance of separation between the White and African American teachers in the school. Mrs. Bethune said the school was taking the necessary steps to correct this:

> We had a meeting and Mrs. Woodson asked faculty members to list the strengths of the school and the weaknesses. Teachers pointed out that the separation of the Black and the White teachers was one of the main weaknesses of the school. We knew that this was a weakness, and Mrs. Woodson was concerned. So we started a team-building program to build community among the teachers. We try to make it so that teachers [Black and White] try to get together a little bit more after school or besides being up here at the school. Some of them try to get together over to each other's houses and things like that.

The effectiveness of the efforts by Mrs. Woodson and Mrs. Bethune hinged on the will of the teachers to make attempts to get to know one another much better. The focus on developing collegiality between Black and White teachers provides insight into the influence of race in shaping the nature of the relationships between teachers from various cultural and ethnic groups. White and Black teachers in St. Louis—like Black and White people in American society—have had different social, historical, and cultural experiences. Therefore, the importance of fostering collegiality among the diverse faculty at Denson would be imperative if these adults hoped to do the same among students from diverse cultural backgrounds.

CONCLUSION

This chapter focused on the factors influencing the decisions of African American parents from one particular St. Louis community to enroll their children in the magnet component of the St. Louis desegregation plan. Those parents who chose the magnet school option had a slightly—but not much—higher socioeconomic status and had greater access to information (i.e., social networks) about the magnet school process than did the other African American parents from the 'Ville. In general, these parents' decisions were not driven by a perceived lack of quality in the predominantly Black neighborhood elementary school; instead, they wanted their children to experience the thematic focus that Denson Magnet School had to offer. However, once African American parents got their children into Denson, they struggled to have a real presence in the school. School personnel acknowledged that the school needed to improve in its efforts to involve these parents.

A key point in the chapter is the role that the African American faculty and staff played in creating a sense of belonging for the African American students and families. These educators, for the most part, took seriously the role they had to play in creating opportunities for the African American children and did not leave this to White educators and parents. This particular finding is important when looking at the experiences of Black children in schools and the persistent achievement gap between Black and White children.

A high-quality teaching force, rigorous academic curriculum, and psychologically welcoming educational setting are critical in the overall effort to effectively educate African American children. However, when educators in urban schools are not proactive in creating such an environment, the chances for many low-income African American children to transcend structural inequalities such as poverty and racism will continue to be few and far between. Inequities will persist for Black children when they have few advocates in a school; this is true even for magnet schools, where diversity is a cornerstone of the school environment and student population.

Therefore, as the educational research and social science communities explore and attempt to understand social processes inside schools, particularly the manner in which the students relate to one another, they cannot ignore the nature of the relationships forged among the professionals within these schools. The interactions among educators from diverse social-class and racial-ethnic backgrounds in schools are as significant as the interactions among students from diverse racial-ethnic backgrounds who attend these schools. As this chapter has highlighted, it is not enough to boast of the value of a racially balanced school when Black children are not equitably and academically benefiting from their attendance at racially balanced schools, the school lacks a racially diverse faculty, and the school personnel are racially divided.

CHAPTER 4

Ambassadors or Sacrificial Lambs? Black Families and Students in a Suburban, White School

When urban, low-income Black students attend predominantly White and suburban schools, do they go as ambassadors of African American people as a whole, or do they serve as "sacrificial lambs" to advance the ideals of integrated schooling? Black children and families were in the forefront of public school desegregation throughout the United States. Vivid images captured Black children such as Ruby Payne in New Orleans and the Little Rock Nine in Arkansas being escorted by the National Guards into schools in the South, as well as the anger on the faces of White people when Black children enrolled in all-White schools in northeastern cities such as Boston.

More than three decades after public school desegregation became enforced and Black children began to attend predominantly White schools, what are Black children's experiences in these schools and low-income Black parents' interactions with school personnel whose racial identities, cultural frameworks, and social-class backgrounds are often vastly different?

This chapter describes the experiences of African American families and students who participated in the transfer part of the St. Louis desegregation plan, specifically focusing on three sets of African American families from the 'Ville whose children attended one particular school in the suburbs—Spring Hill Elementary School. These African American parents made what they thought were the best choices to ensure their children's success in school and, hopefully, in life.

The ethnographic portraits of the families, school, and educators reveal the underlying racial and social-class dynamics within the school, particularly the perilous predicament that low-income Black families and children often face in predominantly White suburban schools. Many of the educators in Spring Hill Elementary School appeared to have genuinely wanted African American transfer students to feel welcomed in the school. However, structural and cultural barriers contributed to the invisibility of Black children and families in the school, the disjuncture between Black parents and White educators' expectations of Black children, and the one-sided power dynamics in the school that ultimately reinforced the hierarchy of White people over Black people.

INSIDE HOMEWOOD AND SPRING HILL ELEMENTARY SCHOOL

"Welcome to Homewood: Population 42,325." This sign can be seen from the main expressway en route to Spring Hill Elementary School. A Kinko's Copy Center, a Pizza Hut, and an array of other small businesses lined the main road in Homewood leading up to the school. In addition to these businesses, the suburban town of Homewood was home to a *Fortune* 500 company that was the second-largest employer in the county—after a medical center. In 2000, the annual median family income was approximately $103,000 and the average price of a home was $262,000. White people made up more than 90 percent of Homewood's residents and African Americans made up approximately 2 percent. Although almost 12 percent of Missouri's residents lived below the poverty level, a little more than 2 percent of Homewood's residents did so.

Some of the nation's fastest-growing businesses were located in Homewood. More than 35 percent of Homewood's residents were college-educated, almost twice the state's average. Spring Hill Elementary School was a reflection of the economic and population growth of the county (the population increased from 28,000 in 1980 to more than 46,000 in 2000); the school was built in 1989 to accommodate the increased student population. During the 1990s, the student population in the district went from 19,000 to about 22,000 students. By the end of the 2006–2007 academic year, the school system's enrollment still hovered around the 22,000 student mark.

The distance to Spring Hill Elementary School from downtown St. Louis was approximately 60 miles round-trip. The school was a red-brick, single-story building, with a campus that encompassed about two city blocks. Before the morning bell rang on one particular day, five to ten White parents quickly made their way into the school to volunteer in the classrooms. Inside the school, a Community Board with news and events hung on the wall; the board listed dates for mammogram screenings, heart disease checking, and diabetes screening. Next to this board was a picture of a little red schoolhouse, informing the visitor of how "Spring Hill strives to be an Effective School." A "Nondiscrimination Statement" was posted on the wall outside the office:

> It is the policy of the Homewood School District not to discriminate on the basis of race, color, creed, sex or disabilities in its education programs, activities or employment practices. Inquiries by students, parents or employees regarding Homewood School District's nondiscrimination policies should be directed to the Compliance Coordinators.

Mrs. Anderson, the head secretary and one of the three White female staff members in the front office, was the first person to greet parents and visitors when they walked into the building. On the wall in the office hung a framed picture and a letter from the former first lady Barbara Bush, as well as posters of the St. Louis skyline, the St. Louis World's Fair in 1904, the St. Louis Symphony, the Art Museum, and the Arch.

Admission Policies

Approximately 700 students were enrolled in Spring Hill Elementary School. Of this number, 640 students were White and residents of Homewood. Fifty African American students from St. Louis transferred into Spring Hill; eleven of the African American students at Spring Hill resided in Homewood. To qualify for their children to attend Spring Hill or a school in any other participating county school district, African American parents in St. Louis were required to fill out application forms for a city-to-county transfer. Parents had to list their top three choices of county school districts. The Voluntary Interdistrict Coordinating Council (VICC) processed all applications. If parents' top three choices were not available, the applications would then be forwarded to alternate school districts.

Faculty Profiles

The faculty at Spring Hill Elementary was predominantly White and female. Out of sixty staff and faculty members, there was one White male teacher and one African American female teacher. The faculty included the principal, Dr. Tolliver; several teachers who had transferred from another school upon the building of Spring Hill; and a group of teachers who began their teaching careers at Spring Hill. Dr. Tolliver had been the principal for seven years.[1] Born in St. Louis, he had also attended school in the University City School District in St. Louis, considered a more "naturally integrated" school district due to its housing patterns at the time.

Dr. Tolliver also taught in the University City School District. He would often talk about how highly he valued that teaching experience because, he said, "Teaching there brought me into daily proximity with African American people." An African American parent, who had one child enrolled in Spring Hill, said that "Dr. Tolliver is used to Black people. His father was a professor at Harris-Stowe [a predominantly Black teachers college in St. Louis] and he raised his children around Black people."

But most of the teachers at Spring Hill had not spent any time around Black people. Their lives differed drastically from the experiences of the St. Louis African American children who transferred into the school. Many of these teachers' spouses worked in the corporations in the county. Some teachers, like Mrs. Henderson, had stopped teaching when their children were young but resumed when they became older. Prior to teaching, Mrs. Henderson noted that she was "very involved and I participated in my children's school a whole lot. Teachers appreciated that. I went in every once in a while and I would read to the children in my children's classroom."

Family Profiles

Approximately 80 percent of the families in Homewood were homeowners (U.S. Census Bureau, 1990, 2000), and many of the parents at Spring Hill Elementary were employed in the corporations and businesses nearby. Some of the mothers were stay-at-home mothers with their younger children. In contrast to the families that resided in Homewood County, the African American families from the 'Ville in St. Louis did not have the types of jobs or receive the income from employment that enabled them to conveniently participate in the affairs of Spring Hill School. Family makeup included a two-parent family in which both parents had some college education, a family comprised of a mother and grandmother, and a single mother. As Table 4.1 reveals, the profiles of these families reveal the daily challenges, stresses, and demands placed on them. However, despite the inherent obstacles as a result of the nature of their work and their economic status, the three sets of African American families from the 'Ville still made choices and sacrifices for their children to attend Spring Hill— hoping for a "good education."

Table 4.1. Spring Hill family profiles, selected African American transfer students.

FAMILY	VILLE COMMUNITY AFFILIATION	OCCUPATION	EDUCATION	YEARS IN THE VILLE COMMUNITY
Camden: Married parents; six children in four different schools; relatives living next door	One child attended Fairmont and the other attended Spring Hill.	Mr. Camden: Construction worker Mrs. Camden: Baggage claim worker at airport	Completed high school and met in college; neither completed college	10
Ross/Aikens: Ms. Ross: Divorced mother; three children, two grandchildren Ms. Aikens: Single parent of two children and Ms. Ross's daughter	Ms. Ross is originally from Ohio. Her three children attended county schools. Ms. Aikens once attended the neighborhood school, Fairmont. Her two children attend Spring Hill.	Ms. Ross: Employed at the local children's hospital	Ms. Ross: Graduated from high school. Ms. Aikens: Attended a county school as part of the desegregation plan, but did not graduate; completing G.E.D.	17
Perry: Single mother; five children	Two older daughters attend St. Louis schools. Two youngest daughters attend Spring Hill. Oldest son once attended a middle school in the county.	Unemployed, receives AFDC (TANF)	Attended St. Louis public schools until 10th grade, but did not graduate from high school	5

AFRICAN AMERICAN PARENTS' REASONS FOR CHOOSING SPRING HILL

Recruitment efforts designed to encourage African American parents to send their children to the county schools were vigorous in St. Louis. Brochures and other sources of information were sent to city school libraries, community centers, churches, laundries, and day-care facilities. Advertisements appeared in newspapers and on television. In addition to these sources of information, parents reported they also found out about Spring Hill by word-of-mouth through conversations with friends or relatives. As Ms. Perry said:

A friend of mine told me about the county schools. Her kids were going to the Homewood School District. She said, "Maybe you would like them going to the Homewood School District." You know how you hear word from somebody else. She said the Homewood School District [Spring Hill's District] was a very good school district, Triple A. Then she told me about it by us staying next door to each other and our children playing together. . . . They would have somebody in the district they know. So I got the applications and they approved it, and then my children started going to the county school.

Ms. Perry's statement is consistent with the study and survey data of parental choice in St. Louis by Goldring and Smrekar (1995), who found that over half of the African American parents who chose the county schools in St. Louis used informal social networks, such as discussions with their friends or relatives, as sources of information. Social networks informed the African American parents about the quality of the education in the county schools, the resources that the schools offered, and students' experiences in the county schools. Choosing the county schools often occurred as a result of these informal networks.

None of the African American parents interviewed visited Spring Hill Elementary prior to signing their children up for the transfer plan. Moreover, the African American parents whose children attended the various county schools often did not visit the schools until they received notification from the VICC that their children had been admitted to a particular school. Ms. Perry further explained how she chose Spring Hill:

Well, I really wanted them to go to a county school. I filled out the paperwork. . . . The people that I sent the form to decided from the paper that you send what school your child could go to. I don't know how they do it; they say, "Well, your kids can go to Spring Hill." Then they sent out this letter and invited me to go and see the school and stuff like that.

Ms. Perry and a grandparent, Ms. Ross, said that their children were having academic problems in the schools in the city and that nothing was being done in St. Louis Public Schools to rectify these problems. They felt that Spring Hill was positioned to do a better job in meeting their children's educational needs than were schools in St. Louis. Ms. Perry elaborated:

I decided to enroll my children in the county school because in the city, they never attempted to find out what my daughter's problem was. Out in the county, they found out what it was. She [her daughter] said they gave her oral tests because they knew that she had a phobia of taking tests.

Ms. Ross's comments echoed those of Ms. Perry:

In the city schools, they never tried to figure out what was wrong with my child. Out in the county school they met the needs of my children. They have diagnosed my grandson as a slow learner. They sent him so that he could be tested.

Both Ms. Perry and Ms. Ross appeared to have been desperate to find out the reasons for their children's academic and social problems prior to sending them to Spring Hill. For them, the St. Louis public schools were not meeting their children's needs. Moreover, they trusted that the school would make the correct assessment, as illustrated by their agreement with the tests/diagnoses administered to their children.

Although three sets of African American parents from the section of the 'Ville community in St. Louis chose to send their children to Spring Hill Elementary, these parents' reasons for choosing the school varied. One particular set of parents' reasons are worth noting. On walking into the Camden family's home, one got a keen sense of an African cultural ethos in the home. They were Rastafarians, and the entire family—parents and six children—wore dreadlocks.[2] Pictures of Marcus Garvey,[3] Haile Selaisse, and African dancers hung on the walls of their home. According to Mr. and Mrs. Camden, they chose different schools for their children for the enriched educational experiences and according to each of their children's particular needs. They also viewed the family rather than the school, as essentially responsible for providing information for their children's cultural development. As Mr. Camden said:

I don't expect the school out there to teach my son about his culture. We do that here at home. I am primarily concerned with what he learns [academically] out there in the school. We will give him the cultural experiences here at home.

All the African American parents interviewed said their decisions to send their children to Spring Hill were greatly influenced by their perception that county schools had more resources than did the city schools:

The county schools, they got computers and everything. My little girl knows a lot about computers. The city schools ain't got nothing! Have you been into a city school before? You go in there and the walls are caving in, and they just don't put nothing into the city schools. I went out to my little girl's school and they have everything out there. The buildings look better than the city schools. These schools in the city are old and run-down. (Ms. Aikens)

I wanted to give them [her children] a better education. They were into computers. Like in the city schools, my kids didn't know nothing about computers. And they work with them much more, much better in the county school district, than they do in the city school district. I found that to be very much true. Like for Denise, when I got her out of the city schools, she couldn't read a lick. She could not read at all. Now she is catching up. (Ms. Perry)

The perception by these African American parents that county schools had more financial resources was not unfounded. In addition to funds that were appropriated for the education of the children in their respective districts, the county school districts were reimbursed for the per-pupil expenditure—equal to the cost of educating children in the district—for those African American students who transferred into their schools. During the 2006–2007 academic year, Homewood School District received $11 million dollars to cover the costs of the approximately 1,857 African American students from St. Louis who transferred into its district. Additionally, the county districts received half of the amount of state aid allocated per child for each of the approximately 1,100 students from their respective districts who transferred into the city's magnet schools.

SCHOOL–FAMILY PARTNERSHIPS: OPPORTUNITIES AND CONSTRAINTS

On any given day of the week, five to ten White parents from Homewood were at Spring Hill Elementary School working as volunteers. Parents participated in every aspect of the school. The PTA meetings, programs, and plays at the school were well attended by parents. Some of these parents, because they did not work outside of the home, had the time and opportunity to visit and to volunteer. Of those parents who worked, many had flexible job schedules that allowed them to attend school events. Rarely were African American parents, on the other hand, present in the school. Impediments to African American parents' participation in the school seemed to hinge on several factors.

According to teachers, the lack of adequate transportation was one of the primary reasons why African American parents were not involved at Spring Hill. In survey data of the African American parents who participated in the St. Louis desegregation plan, half of them identified transportation as their greatest need for attendance at school meetings and functions.[4] Below, the principal and a teacher at Spring Hill Elementary School further described the impact that the lack of transportation had on African American parents' participation in the school:

> I think we would like to have those parents involved. The parents out in the county, they are involved. We have several situations in which we have tried to get the parents from the city to get out here [to the school]. We have offered to have cabs to go down or buses to go down. Their biggest problem is trying to get transportation out here; it's not that they don't have the desire. We've tried on several occasions to have transportation provided. (Dr. Tolliver)

> Because of transportation, the city parents are not as involved. I can't think of any of the parents out here that would not have transportation; that makes it difficult for the city parents. The parents out here can walk if they want to. We had this one parent that wanted to be active; she wanted to go to Jefferson City with us. But we don't have the resources. I promised her that I would get her out here. (Mrs. Henderson)

The lack of reliable transportation was not the only obstacle; the distance and work schedules, according to parents, prevented them from actively participating in the school. For low-income parents, the distance to the school was a persistent obstacle:

> I don't have no car, and I can't get out there to the schools. If you take a cab, it's like the school is out of town. That's one of the reasons why I can't go. See, I had a car, but it's not running at this time; so, I'm not able to make it up there much. (Ms. Perry)

> I wished that I had more time to go out there to see my child's teacher. It's hard for me to make it because I pull a double shift. I don't have as much time to go out there to the school. (Mrs. Camden)

The secretary, Mrs. Anderson, reiterated how these obstacles limited African American parents' presence in the school:

Many of the parents in the city have distance as an issue, and a lot of them work night hours and can't take a day off. The parents out here might be the owner of a business and can schedule appropriately, or might be at home and not working. So they can schedule time to be off. St. Louis does not have a good county-to-city transportation system either. A good portion of the city parents do not have transportation. That is tough on them; all would like to come out more than they do.

At the annual parent appreciation tea, there were 2 African American parents among the approximately 150 parents present. One of these parents was from St. Louis and the other lived in Homewood near Spring Hill Elementary. The lack of African American parents' presence during this event spoke to the impact that time constraints, distance, and the lack of reliable transportation had on these parents' involvement at Spring Hill. But what does this say about those few African American parents who lived in Homewood? It seems that more of them would have been present at this event because they, unlike most African American parents from St. Louis, would have had more flexible work schedules.

On another occasion, when two African American parents at a school event were asked about the small number of African American parents present, one parent responded, "I'm lucky that I came out here. I have five children at home, so I rarely have the time to come way out here." On this particular occasion, the school had paid for these two parents to take taxis out to the school.[5]

Dr. Tolliver, the principal, felt that the transfer program should have been modified to provide transportation for parents to attend events in the county schools:

> I think the voluntary desegregation program can do a better job in providing opportunities for the children's parents to come out here. It is very difficult to find transportation. They get the students out here, but when it comes to the parents coming out here, they [the transfer plan] don't have any funds.

Mrs. Albert, a teacher at Spring Hill, illustrated the consequences of African American parents' inability to attend programs and events in which their children were involved:

> For example, there was a little boy who wanted his parents to come out here to watch him participate in a program out here. I offered to stay out here with him; unfortunately, they got lost on

their way out here and he missed his part. But at least he was able to do the second part. He was crushed! His mother said, "Baby I'm sorry that I got lost."

Due to time, transportation, and job constraints, the parents of the African American children who transferred into Spring Hill missed many of the programs and events that were scheduled at the school. In contrast, many of the Homewood parents had spouses and flexible schedules that allowed them to choose when to work—or choose to remain at home:

Does it make you a better parent if you can get out here to activities and events because it is easier to get here? I don't think so. We have some parents with teaching degrees and are choosing to stay at home. Those are wonderful parents because they have been trained as teachers. . . . I would assume that most of my city parents work, or they are at home with small children. Where out here, a lot of my parents don't work and they are at the school full time; they are more accessible. (Mrs. Henderson, teacher)

Many policy makers, professional organizations, researchers, and educators cite parental influence as a central pillar of student success (Epstein, 1992; Ingram, Wolfe, & Lieberman, 2007; Sanders, 2008) and a reason why some achieve—even before they begin school (see Lareau, 2003). Clearly, parents' educational attainment, child-rearing practices, socioeconomic status, and access to learning opportunities have an impact on academic performance throughout children's K–12 schooling and beyond (Lareau, 2003). As highlighted by the constraints to Black parents' involvement at Spring Hill—manifested in the lack of transportation to and from the school—poverty played an integral role in the extent to which these African American parents from St. Louis were able to participate in the school. It is imperative to have appropriate support structures in place to involve African American parents in the school if their children are to have some semblance of academic success while they are there.

SPRING HILL AND THE INVISIBILITY OF BLACK PEOPLE

There existed a strong partnership between Spring Hill Elementary School's educators and the families who lived in the predominantly White communities surrounding the school. This partnership, however, did not include the African American parents from the neighborhoods in St. Louis. Spring Hill sent out a monthly newsletter to all parents that informed and provided them with the dates and times of important events for the school-year. In this newsletter, parents were informed of the developments during the most recent PTA meetings; dates of events and activities were also listed. Communication with most Spring Hill parents occurred by telephone, newsletters, flyers, and reports sent home. Teachers sent letters home to parents every six weeks informing them of occurrences at the school. With the advent of electronic mail, some of the parents and teachers began to send memos by e-mail as well.

There also were planned parent–teacher conferences twice a year. The parents who were not able to make it to these conferences could contact the teacher later by telephone or e-mail. Of the three families from the 'Ville, two reported that they went to the school to participate in conferences; the other parent conferred by telephone. These parents stated that they rarely visited the school to meet with the teachers. Communication with them, in general, was limited to memos, flyers, and newsletters:

> It is hard for some of the [African American] parents to make it out here. Also, contacting parents at times by telephone might be a problem because some of the parents in the city don't have telephones, or their telephone might be disconnected. (Mrs. Anderson, the secretary)

The African American families who sent their children to Spring Hill were primarily low-income to working-class parents. Of the three families, one of the mothers received Aid to Families with Dependent Children (AFDC; now Temporary Assistance to Needy Families [TANF]). Another family consisted of two working parents who were raising six children; finally, there was a family that included a grandmother who was the sole provider for her daughter and her grandchildren. These families were struggling financially to provide the bare necessities. The limited communication between African American families and Spring Hill faculty and staff magnified the tension during the times that school personnel had to contact the African American parents. Contact was often initiated when there was some disciplinary action that had to be taken against the children:

> I went out there when my child got into some trouble. They wanted to suspend him, and I drove all of the way out there. When I got out there, the teacher acted like she was scared of me. I guess she thought that I was going to come up in there talking ghetto. I don't know why she acted like that. She thought oh little bitty me was going to jump on her! (Mrs. Camden)

Mrs. Long, a teacher, reiterated the nature of the communication between teachers and African American parents:

> We rarely get the chance to talk with our city parents. . . . I hate to say it, but usually the times we talk with them are in negative situations such as when their child has gotten into some trouble.

Effective relations between school personnel and families cannot occur if communication occurs primarily under negative conditions. This lack of communication fostered distrust between the teachers and the African American parents. The following dialogue between me and Mrs. Mitchell (a fifth-grade teacher and the only African American teacher in the school) illustrates the school's fragile relationship with African American parents. Mrs. Mitchell had been a teacher for the past 16 years in the district. After transferring to Spring Hill in 1989, she became the director of SHARP (School, Home, At-Risk Program), which involved working with African American transfer students and their families. SHARP, which was funded through a grant from the state of Missouri, allowed Mrs. Mitchell to work with the African American children who transferred into Spring Hill.

The exchange with Mrs. Mitchell provides further insight into why African American students and families were invisible participants in the Spring Hill community. Mrs. Mitchell juxtaposed Spring Hill's failure to actively involve African American parents in the school with the efforts by school personnel at her own child's school (her child attended another county school):

> MORRIS: Was there an effort at your son's school to get the African American parents involved?
> MITCHELL: Yes, more than there was here at Spring Hill.
> MORRIS: Was the school closer into the city?
> MITCHELL: No, it was actually closer to where I live. I don't know if it was just the people or the administration in there [her child's school] that was different; it was just very different. When I did SHARP, we made sure that the [African American] parents had transportation. We went into the city and made sure that the parents came out here. Since funding ended for that program, nothing has happened to try to reach out to the students and their parents.

As the former director of SHARP, Mrs. Mitchell felt that Spring Hill staff and faculty could have done more to develop stronger relationships with the African American families from the city. The discontinuation of SHARP did little to improve the situation; indeed, it created a further disjuncture between the school's faculty and staff and the experiences of the African American students who transferred into the school from the city. Consequently, the type of support for these families, when it did occur, appeared paternalistic, often involving the school having to do something for the "less fortunate" Black children.

PATERNALISM OR SUPPORT FOR BLACK FAMILIES?

Spring Hill Elementary established committees that dealt with issues facing families and teachers, such as the birth of a child or the death of a loved one. There was the Circle of Concerns Committee that made baskets during the holidays and distributed these baskets to parents. During the holiday season in December, the school contacted the African American parents from the city and offered to donate items that they might need. At times, some of these parents were very appreciative about receiving the items from the school. At other times, parents were ambivalent. The responses from the two parents below capture the different reactions:

> During Christmas time, the teachers called my house—I was at work—and asked my oldest daughter if we needed anything. My daughter gave them a list of some things. They really try to help you out; not that I'm so poor and everything, but they helped me out because there were some things that I really needed. (Ms. Ross)

> They came down here and brought some things to me for Christmas. They asked me for a list of things that I might need such as clothes, food, and stuff like that. At first, I didn't want nothing because you don't want people thinking you be begging or nothing like that. I went ahead and took some of the things. They came down here in a big truck and delivered some things. But the funny thing about it was that they brought some policemen with them [*laughs*]. I laughed because it was funny with them bringing a policeman with them. Nobody was going to mess with them. I guess they are scared of Black people or think somebody is going to rob them. (Ms. Perry)

Ms. Perry found it amusing that school personnel presumed that the community in which she lived was filled with criminals. Mrs. Simmons, also a teacher at Spring Hill, stated that "They [police officers] went there [to the predominantly Black neighborhoods with school personnel] because the areas some of our city kids live in are rough." Although this was the rationale given for taking the police officers along, for parents like Ms. Perry, it also conveyed a misunderstanding of the communities from which the students came.

In addition, the delivery of food and clothing, primarily during the holiday season—no matter how well meant—is suggestive of paternalism. The African American parents and students definitely needed financial support. However, these parents also needed support in other ways, most notably in securing transportation to attend their children's school during activities and events. Black families' need for supporting structures in the school to assist in their children's education is one issue that is probably best addressed at the district level. Another major concern involved African American families' and White teachers' different academic expectations of Black children.

Teachers' and Parents' Different Expectations

In general, teachers at Spring Hill believed that the majority of the African American students transferring into the school were not academically prepared. Simultaneously, the African American parents expressed high academic expectations for their children. The following recollection by Ms. Aikens, a parent, highlights how she felt that her concern about her child was misconstrued as anger directed toward the teacher:

> I went up to the school and asked a teacher about my child's grade. He received a grade of a D, and I thought that he could do better. One teacher called another and told her that I was upset. I told him [the principal, Dr. Tolliver] that I was not upset at him but that I wanted to help my child. It's not that the teachers have the problem—my son has the problem. "You have your education, but he has to get his."

Despite her son's grade, Ms. Aikens still believed that he could do better; she placed the responsibility for academic success on her son rather than on the teachers and the school.

In the following excerpted interview, Ms. Perry, an African American parent, vividly describes the different views of a teacher and a parent about the academic ability of an African American student. The teacher believed the student was not prepared for first grade, and she wanted to retain her in kindergarten. However, Ms. Perry was willing to work during the summer months to prepare her daughter for the first grade:

Ms. PERRY: My youngest child is in kindergarten, and their [the school's] kindergarten program is only half a day. They told me they want her to repeat kindergarten now; the teacher feels she might fail. The teacher said "Well, she is doing real well now, but she is just now at the level the other kids were when they first came in." It was the way she was telling me; she really doesn't know, but there is a chance she might not fail.

MORRIS: So you didn't know how to take exactly what she was saying?

Ms. PERRY: Right! I told her, "Why would I send her way back out there for half a day of kindergarten when I could send her down here [to the neighborhood school] for a full day?" What else is she going to learn different from now if she goes back out there for just a half a day? I told the teacher that I don't understand. . . . I feel like this: If my daughter fails the first grade, then she just fails. But I feel as though she is telling me that she has progressed a whole lot. To me that is telling me that she probably could pass the first grade. The teacher doesn't know how much my daughter can gain in the summertime. The teacher told me, "Well, she might not gain that much within the summertime." To me, a few months in the summer is like a semester in school. I told the teacher that I was going to be working with my daughter so that she can catch up.

Ms. Perry felt that she received mixed messages from the teacher rather than just a direct suggestion that her daughter repeat kindergarten. Consequently, Ms. Perry interpreted the teacher's statement to mean that her daughter could go on to first grade, but with some preparation. On the other hand, the teacher appeared to think that there was no possibility that Ms. Perry's daughter would be prepared for first grade.

Mrs. Henderson, a teacher at Spring Hill, offered her perception of teachers' expectations for the African American children in the school. Initially, Mrs. Henderson stated that the teachers had lower expectations for African American students in comparison to the White students. She later modified her statement by saying that the expectations were different; she implicitly attributed this difference to socioeconomic differences between the African American students and the students who live in the county:

I think we have lower expectations for the city kids. Well, they are different but not lower. Is it fair for me to judge a child that turns in a project written on a laser printer the same as one done on a handwritten paper? So is that fair?

Cultural Disregard

A number of scholars have written extensively on how schools and teachers invalidate the cultural experiences of African American students (Delpit, 1996; Foster, 1995; Irvine, 1990; Ladson-Billings, 1994). Irvine (1990) further argues that there is usually a lack of cultural synchronization in schools that inhibits African American students' school success. The absence of an African American cultural presence at Spring Hill created a situation in which African American children had to adjust to a setting that was culturally, racially, and economically different from the world in which they lived. This was further complicated by the fact that there was only one African American teacher in the school, Mrs. Mitchell. And Mrs. Mitchell lived in Homewood, not in St. Louis.

A nondiscrimination policy and the following statement on the wall in the teachers' lounge captured Spring Hill's purported effort to provide an effective education for all its students, despite the backgrounds of the teachers and the majority of the students who attended the school:

> Our task is to provide an education for the kinds of kids we have. Not the kinds of kids we used to have, or want to have. Or the kinds of kids that exist in our minds.

Mrs. Long, a teacher at Spring Hill, offered her view of the importance of valuing and validating students who come from different cultural and economic backgrounds:

> I think that it is important that we know they are coming from a different culture and background. They have areas that we might not know, and they are coming into a whole new culture; and we are sending them back to their home, which is a whole different culture. So academically we've got a lot of things to work through.

Were these statements and policies translated into practices? When asked, in what ways Spring Hill recognized the cultural experiences of African American students, two teachers responded as follows:

> We do a token Black History Month: Frederick Douglass, Martin Luther King, Dr. George Washington Carver. Well, we have been

fortunate to have Mrs. Mitchell here. She has served as a liaison for us. She found resources to bring families out here. (Mrs. Albert)

The first two years it [Black History Month] was done, but we have not done anything in the past few years. It is done on more of an individual basis. There is nothing done from the school's perspective to encourage this. (Mrs. Simmons)

Black History Month can be an opportunity for a school to recognize the cultural heritage and legacy of African American students. However, no recognition of this major African American heritage month took place at Spring Hill. The teachers had the option of deciding whether they wanted to recognize Black History Month in their classrooms. Instead, few teachers celebrated or recognized African American holidays in their classrooms. There were no displays, assemblies, or programs celebrating Dr. Martin Luther King's birthday, Kwanzaa, or Black History Month.

In addition to the teachers' lack of recognition of African American students' cultural holidays and celebrations, there was no overall commitment on the part of the school to celebrate and recognize the numerous accomplishments of African Americans. Mrs. Mitchell, the only African American teacher in the school for several years, worked alone to organize Black History Month celebrations and assemblies for the entire school. Eventually, she found the job was "too much for one person to do."

The nonrecognition of Black History Month and other African American celebrations is symbolic of the school's lack of commitment to creating a culturally enriching educational experience for its Black student population. In contrast, Spring Hill faculty, staff, and students participated in a year-long activity entitled "Celebrate America." The front hallways of the school were draped with red, white, and blue decorations. A bulletin board in the cafeteria included, among other items, pictures of the types of clothing worn by the various presidents of the United States. The "Celebrate America" celebration was not multicultural in nature; instead, this event primarily focused on White Americans' contributions to the United States.

Black Students' Adjustments and Resistance

When schools make very little effort to include the cultural experiences of African American students, those students begin to realize that the experiences that they bring into the school are not valued. Consequently, some African American students may have difficulty adjusting to the norms of the school, thereby inhibiting their school success. According to many of the teachers at Spring Hill, some of the African American students experienced coping "problems" immediately upon transferring to Spring Hill and primarily interacted with other African American transfer students. Teachers also stated that the African American students did not trust the teachers when they first transferred into Spring Hill. According to Dr. Tolliver, these issues were more pronounced for those students who transferred at later grades: "When the older students came out here, they would be more cautious in trusting us."

Some of the teachers agreed that the age at which some African American students transferred to Spring Hill was a major reason they did not adjust as readily to the school environment:

> I can tell you when it is best. It is better when the children come out here in the earlier grades, and they overlook the boundaries. But it seems when they are in the fifth grade that you have more noticing of differences from students coming out here [later, compared to those who came earlier]. (Mrs. Long, teacher)

> The sooner they come out here they get kind of used to the routine that is going on. When they come out here like in fourth or fifth grade, the attitude situation is a little bit different, and the way they react to things is a little stronger. They wait to see what people are going to do. It is a little bit harder because they don't know how this school operates. (Mrs. Simmons, teacher)

In contrast to these views, Mrs. Mitchell, the African American teacher, attributed the difficulties experienced by the African American students to their being in a predominantly White and middle class suburban school:

> I had to shift the focus of SHARP so that it would deal with the problems the Black children were having out here in the school, such as behavior problems. This was a new environment and many of the students were not used to being in an all-White environment.

What are the underlying reasons for some of the teachers' perceptions regarding older African American students transferring into Spring Hill? Could it be that these older students were more cognizant and perceptive of the dynamics of race in the school, in comparison to the younger students? Moreover, were the older students more resistant to the White cultural framework that they encountered when they transferred into

Spring Hill? While the teachers often felt that the older African American children did not trust them, these same teachers had already demonstrated to the African American students that they did not trust Black people and the residents of their communities. Consequently, these educators and school personnel took police officers with them when they ventured into the St. Louis communities where the African American students lived. Thus, the African American children already knew that the White teachers did not trust them without it ever being said.

As noted earlier, approximately 10 percent of Spring Hill's African American student population also resided in the city of Homewood. Their experiences at Spring Hill were somewhat different because of the social-class differences between them and the African American students from St. Louis. Some of the teachers said that the African American students who transferred into Spring Hill usually labeled the African American students who resided in Homewood as trying to "act White":

> I have a little African American boy who lives out here. He is a very good student. . . . They [African American transfer students] tease him because he lives out here. They tease him about "acting White." The city kids are the ones that will usually push away. They don't want to associate with the Black kids [in the county] that they perceive to be "acting White." (Mrs. Albert, teacher)

John Ogbu (1978, 1990, 2003) contended that some African American students develop certain secondary cultural traits as a defense mechanism against an imposing dominant culture. Thus, many of them have associated academic success with White people and consequently have accused some of their African American peers as "acting White." In predominantly White and racially desegregated schools, African American students are most likely to attach this term to those African American students they perceive to be emulating the values, language, style, and culture of White Americans. For example, Prudence Carter (2005) found that low-income African American youth did not racialize being smart, doing well in school, or getting good grades. Instead of being associated with academic achievement, "acting White" was associated with a set of styles and symbolic vehicles, such as speech and dress styles. And those high-achieving students who were considered to be "acting White" were enrolled in Advanced Placement courses and, therefore, spent a considerable amount of their school time around their White peers.

Thus, it could be that the Black students in Homewood shared similar tastes (language, music, and dress) with many of their White classmates who were middle-class and also lived in Homewood. Moreover, the animosity that some of the African American transfer students directed at the few Black students who resided in Homewood might also have been a result of their recognition of the class-based hierarchical structure of the school (see Tyson, Darity, & Castellino, 2005). In essence, they might have seen the few Black students who resided in Homewood as privileged. Barriers persisted in the school—across and within race and social class. The clear manifestation of this chasm was the euphemistic reference to the African American transfer students from St. Louis as "city kids."

City Kids

The African American students who transferred into Spring Hill were re-ferred to as the "city kids." Mr. Camden, an African American father who once drove a taxi to transfer the African American children, noted:

> I would have to take Black children out to the county schools. They [the Homewood students] referred to the African American students as "city kids." That means they treated the Black children out there like second-class citizens or visitors. They are not welcomed, but tolerated.

Mrs. Camden reiterated her husband's view:

> I went through a point when they were out there and we had this problem where, not necessarily getting called a nigger, but they were getting called the "deseg children" or the "city kids." They had labeled these children, and I had to go up there and basically just clown. I told the principal that my child has a name, a given name; he is a person. Don't attach these labels to these children. Don't do that! Basically, what the [White] children were saying is that the children that were on the bus were poor and Black.

Rather than refer to the African American transfer students as "Afri-can American" or "Black," White teachers and students used the euphe-mism "city kids" to refer to these students. This labeling depersonalized the African American students' experiences at Spring Hill. Race was de-emphasized and teachers, for the most part, embraced a "color-blind" dis-course when relating to the African American students. As Ladson-Billings (1994) suggests, an attempt at this type of color-blindness "masks a 'dys-conscious racism,' an uncritical habit of mind that justifies inequity" (p. 31). Individuals might not consciously do this. Some do not want to feel guilty or embarrassed by categorizing students into certain racial categories.

However, the failure to acknowledge African American students' particular cultures and ethnicities ignores the ways in which some students are privileged and others are disadvantaged in classrooms, schools, and society. These privileges and disadvantages were very pronounced in the power dynamic in the relationships between the White students and both the few African American students from Homewood and those who had transferred in from St. Louis.

White Hosts and Black Students

Teachers and parents from Homewood sometimes served as host families for African American students who participated in after-school and extracurricular activities. Ms. Aikens, a parent, shared her enthusiasm for the families serving as hosts for her child:

> I think that it is a great idea. The host families are great. My son spent the night with families in the county school. Chris is excited. He always reminds me four or five times that he is going to spend the night. Some of the families even bring him to our door.

Ms. Aikens was very appreciative of how some of the White host families embraced her child, particularly because she did not normally expect White families to display such generosity. The other African American parents said that there were times when their children spent the night with host families but were not brought home by them. Instead, their children would catch the bus and ride back to their neighborhoods. Although there were some instances in which the White host families took the students home, the Black parents indicated that this was not usually the case. Most of the time, their children would take the school bus back to their neighborhoods after spending the night with host families.

Reciprocal-exchange opportunities between White students and African American students were nonexistent. Parents and teachers knew of no instances in which White students from Homewood County had spent the night in African American students' homes. Brochures that advertised the transfer program included photographs of African American students in the county schools, in the county communities, or visiting the White students' homes. None of them depicted White students in the homes of the African American students who lived in St. Louis.

By not visiting and spending time in the African American students' communities, the White students did not have the opportunity to fully experience the day-to-day lives of the African American students. In a sense, this situation suggests that African American students could benefit from spending time with White students in the county but there was little that the White students could gain from visiting and spending time in the African American students' homes and communities. Such arrangements—though perhaps well intentioned at times—created an imbalance of power in how African American families and children interacted with the White teachers, parents, and children. All the activities occurred in the county school, homes, and communities, which was convenient for the White students and families.

Finally, what impact did the visits to the White students' homes have on the African American students? A statement by a teacher, Mrs. Albert, suggests that after some of the African American students spent the night in teachers' and families' homes in the county, the students began wishing they possessed some of the material things the White children in the county had:

> I had a little boy who said "I wished so bad that we had some of the things the children out here have—like a nice home." He always came home asking his mother why he didn't have that. His mother didn't know how to deal with that. This is an isolated incident; I don't know if that is always the case.

This was not an isolated case. Mr. Camden, a parent, said his son "went out to the county schools and saw the nice houses out there and asked us if we could have a home like theirs."

In closing, some African American parents chose Spring Hill based on a perception that the predominantly White county schools had more resources and were safer than schools in the city. These parents' choices were more likely to have been considered if the particular county school district was in need of more African American students to reach its African American student enrollment goal. Unfortunately, many of the African American parents who wanted their children to attend the predominantly White and suburban schools did not visit the schools prior to their children's attendance there. For these parents, having the means and time to visit the county schools was a problem. Some of the suburban school districts were at least 30 to 40 minutes away from the communities in St. Louis. Only after the district office that was responsible for coordinating the transfer part of the desegregation plan assigned children to a specific school were African American parents then offered a one-time taxi fare to go to the county schools to register their children. There were no funds available to allow parents to visit districts of interest and, therefore, enable them to make more informed choices. These parents, for the most part, *chose any predominantly White and suburban school* or accepted the suburban school that was assigned to their children.

Once in the suburban schools, there were very few instances in which the faculty and staff developed genuine relationships with the African American parents from St. Louis. At Spring Hill Elementary, staff and faculty professed a sincere interest in developing relationships; however, this was not evident in their actions and school practices. Rather than take proactive steps to ensure that meaningful partnerships were developed and maintained with the African American families, the faculty and staff embraced a laissez-faire approach. The efforts on the part of the only African American teacher in the school, Mrs. Mitchell, were undermined by the lack of state funding for a program that focused on strengthening the relationship between Spring Hill's faculty and African American families from the city.

Distance, the lack of transportation, and inflexible work schedules were also obstacles that prevented African American parents from regularly visiting the school. These obstacles were viewed as an issue for the interdistrict transfer plan to address, rather than an issue for the particular school or the school district to rectify. Consequently, African American students' experiences in schools like Spring Hill were fraught with misunderstandings, labeling, and the devaluing of the African American cultural experience in the following manner: (1) African American students were labeled as "city kids"; (2) there was a lack of African American adult presence in the school; (3) a paternalistic approach toward African Americans best characterized the relationship between school personnel and African American families and students; and (4) the school provided only a token recognition of African American students' cultural heritage. Although low-income African American students from St. Louis were physically present in the school, they were *invisible* when it came to having a role in the school. The students were bused in at the beginning of the schoolday and then bused out at the end of the day.

To revisit the question posed at the beginning of this chapter: Are African American students who attend predominantly White schools ambassadors for their people or sacrificial lambs? First, ambassadorship implies a reciprocal relationship in which two groups—with some degree of equality and power—come together for a shared goal and understanding. Representatives from each group may spend time in the other group's setting with the understanding that there will be a cross-cultural exchange. The experiences of African American students who transferred into the predominantly White suburban schools reflected more of a sacrificial relationship. As the findings from Spring Hill Elementary School reveal, there was never a reciprocal relationship because of the lack of a true desire for mutual understanding. Black people took the steps to reach out, but White people did not reciprocate. They received the African American children not as equals but as inferiors. Moreover, the school setting also bred animosity between Black students who lived in St. Louis and those who lived in Homewood because White people decided which African American students would be their "good" Black students.

PART III

Quality Schooling in the New Black Metropolis: Possibilities and Dilemmas

CHAPTER 5

Out of Nazareth? Promise in Central-City Schools

Historically, Black people in the United States have drawn parallels between their social and historical conditions and those of oppressed people in the Bible (Cone, 1970/1990; West, 1982). Most contemporary accounts of urban and predominantly African American schools and communities are reminiscent of the biblical Nazareth (which was considered a poor, neglected, and despised area) and the conventional historical view of all-Black schools during the era of legalized segregation. These depictions encompass sordid images of dilapidated buildings, inferior teaching, and inadequate resources and supplies.

In particular, recent accounts of urban and predominantly African American schools and communities describe them as "concentrated areas of poverty," created in part by the disappearance of industries from urban centers (Wilson, 1996), inadequate funding (Kozol, 1991), school district and governmental neglect (Anyon, 1997), and the dismantling of desegregation (Boger & Orfield, 2005).

Although these accounts highlight the structural inequalities facing urban and predominantly African American schools, an unfortunate consequence of this representation of urban schooling has been the generic depiction of the schools and the educators who work in them as noncaring and academically deficient. They are depicted, together with African American people and culture, as inferior and deficit-oriented. Such depictions provide a partial view of these schools and communities at the dawn of the 21st century and rarely capture the agency that has historically been demonstrated by predominantly African American schools and educators in response to persistent structural inequalities.

For instance, over the past three decades a body of scholarship has emerged that offers a different picture of Black schooling during legalized segregation and illuminates the integral role that all-Black schools played in educating Black students in the midst of legalized racism (e.g., Anderson, 1988; Cecelski, 1994; Jones, 1981; Morris & Morris, 2002; Perry, 2003; Savage, 1998; Siddle Walker, 1996, 2000). Despite the gross inequalities in the distribution of resources and the unresponsiveness to the needs of Black students by all-White school boards and state officials, some Black schools boasted strong reputations for providing an exemplary education (Jones, 1981), possessed stable faculties and administrators who connected the school with the Black community (Jones, 1981; Siddle Walker, 1996), served as focal points for community and church activities, and played an integral role in solidifying Black communities (Cecelski, 1994; Morris & Morris, 2002; Siddle Walker, 1996).

Schools that serve mostly low-income and African American children have patterns of low academic performance. But scholars and policy makers must not intentionally suppress the stories of those schools that are high achieving out of fear that highlighting them in our scholarship represents a retreat from *Brown*. The reality is that public schools are segregated without having to make such an assertion. Given that millions of African American students will continue to attend predominantly African American schools in central cities, presented are ethnographic descriptions of two African American elementary schools that successfully educated the students they served. These two schools are not presented as a panacea for urban Black education but to understand under what circumstances some urban and predominantly Black schools have succeeded with their students.

Fairmont Elementary School in St. Louis had one of the highest student attendance rates in the city and consistently outperformed students in the St. Louis public school system, including magnet schools, on traditional measures such as standardized tests. In 1997, U.S. Secretary of Education Richard Riley recognized Fairmont Elementary School as one of 100 schools in the United States with outstanding Title I programs. On the other hand, Lincoln Elementary School in Atlanta was one of 11 elementary schools in 1997 selected as a "Georgia School of Excellence," based on a combination of factors that included student attendance rates and standardized test scores, the curriculum, and parent participation rates.

The initial phase of the investigation of Fairmont Elementary School, Denson Magnet School, and Spring Hill Elementary Schools was drawn from a multicity (St. Louis, Cincinnati, and Nashville) research study of magnet and neighborhood schools to examine the impact of public school choice on the development and maintenance of school community.[1] Fairmont Elementary School was selected for in-depth investigation after African American educators in the city and the school repeatedly suggested that the school be considered for further study because of its academic reputation and what they defined as a "strong connection" with African American families and the nearby community.

Survey data from a multicity study affirmed these educators' assertions about Fairmont. The most frequent response that parents surveyed gave for choosing Fairmont was its proximity to their homes. The second most frequent response was the school's academic reputation. More than 90 percent of the parents surveyed "strongly agreed" or "agreed" that the school created opportunities for parents to be involved. The other two schools (Denson Magnet School and Spring Hill Elementary School) were chosen because they also enrolled students from the Fairmont attendance zone.

From 1994 through 1997, intensive ethnographic research took place in Fairmont Elementary School, Denson Magnet School, and Spring Hill Elementary School.[2] This phase of the research investigation specifically focused on how public school desegregation shaped the relationship among schools, families, and communities. The research in Atlanta, on the other hand, provided a different context, one in which desegregation was not the district's policy. Atlanta's public school system, which abandoned its desegregation plan during the early 1970s, was the site for the second phase of the research project.

Lincoln Elementary School in the Atlanta public school system was purposefully sampled, based on its reputation for playing a key role in the nearby community. In the fall of 1998, a director of an urban educational research project at a local university (Folami Prescott-Adams) initially suggested the school as a possible site. Folami had a strong reputation for her involvement with African American "grassroots" efforts in Atlanta. Moreover, newspaper articles occasionally featured the school and the principal's accomplishments. In informal conversations with African American residents from the community, it became clear that many concurred that Lincoln Elementary School maintained a strong relationship with the community. Additional suggestions from African American educators in the Atlanta public school system attributed Lincoln's reputation to the principal, Dr. Frazier.

An African American female, Dr. Frazier (who unexpectedly passed away in the spring of 1999) was renowned for partnering the school with businesses and community-based agencies.[3] In addition, Lincoln was one of 11 elementary schools selected as a "Georgia School of Excellence," based on a combination of factors that included student attendance rates and standardized test scores, the curriculum, and parent participation rates. The academic performance of Black students at Fairmont and Lincoln is a function of the relationship between the adults and the children in the schools and between the school and the families.

For example, Black students at Fairmont Elementary School exceeded the achievement levels of Black students in St. Louis City schools. Moreover, Fairmont's students generally outperformed the Black students at Denson Magnet School and Spring Hill Elementary School on standardized measures of achievement, as measured by the percentage of Black students meeting annual proficiency targets across subject areas. Table 5.1 provides longitudinal achievement test data on reading (communication arts) and math over a 3-year period (2001–2004) for Black students attending the St. Louis area schools in the study. On the reading and math tests, the mean percentage of Fairmont's Black students meeting the annual proficiency targets exceeded that of Black students attending St. Louis City Schools. During two of these years, 2001–2003, the mean percentage of Fairmont's Black students meeting the math targets exceeded that of Denson's and Spring Hill's Black students. In reading, Fairmont's Black students outperformed Spring Hill's Black students in each of the three years. In all three

Table 5.1. Test scores of African American students, St. Louis area schools.

	Mean Test Scores	
School or District	Communication Arts (Target: 18.4)	Math (Target: 8.3)
2001–2002 Academic Year		
Fairmont	25.5	35.1
St. Louis City Schools	13.9	8.9
Denson Magnet	33.3	15.4
Spring Hill	12.5	30.0
	Communication Arts (Target: 19.4)	Math (Target: 9.3)
2002–2003 Academic Year		
Fairmont	39.1	34.1
St. Louis City Schools	12.7	10.3
Denson Magnet	19.6	24.6
Spring Hill	13.3	31.0
	Communication Arts (Target: 20.4)	Math (Target: 10.3)
2003–2004 Academic Year		
Fairmont	25.0	29.8
St. Louis City Schools	14.8	14.5
Denson Magnet	58.2	50.0
Spring Hill	20.0	43.8

Source: Missouri Department of Elementary and Secondary Education Core Data as submitted by Missouri Public Schools (retrieved August 7, 2008, from http://dese.mo.gov /index.html).

years, Fairmont's Black students and Denson's Black students met the annual proficiency targets across all subject areas. While they met the target each year in math, Spring Hill's Black students failed to meet the annual proficiency targets in reading during 2001–2004.

Furthermore, the average Black student at Lincoln Elementary School in Atlanta, Georgia, generally outperformed the average Atlanta Public School System Black student on achievement tests. Table 5.2 shows longitudinal achievement data for Black students at Lincoln compared to Black students across the Atlanta Public School System during 2001–2002, 2003–2004, and 2004–2005. In reading, English, and math, the mean percentage of Lincoln Black students meeting the expected performance level exceeded that of Black students across the Atlanta Public School System.[4]

The relationship that educators at Fairmont and Lincoln built with families and students was each school's foundation for cultivating an academic achievement ethos for Black students. The relationships served as a requisite to academic achievement by fostering a sense of trust and a bond necessary for promoting children's academic achievement. When low-income African American families are disconnected from schools, and educators are disconnected from families and communities, opportunities to forge social and cultural capital became few and far between. Thus,

Table 5.2. Test scores of African American students, Atlanta area schools.

	Mean Test Scores		
School or District	Reading	English	Math
2001–2002 Academic Year			
Lincoln Elementary	78	74	62
Atlanta schools	74	70	63
2003–2004 Academic Year			
Lincoln Elementary	86	92	77
Atlanta schools	72	78	72
2004–2005 Academic Year			
Lincoln Elementary	92	90	74
Atlanta schools	80	83	75

Sources: Georgia School Council Institute, Office of Education Accountability Report Cards (retrieved August 7, 2008, from http://www.gsci.org/ReportCenter/reportcenter.jsp); Governor's Office of Student Achievement (retrieved August 7, 2008, from http://gaosa.org /Report.aspx).

opportunities to build on the knowledge that children bring from home become limited.

The existence of strong relationships (communal bonds) is not the only criteria for academic achievement, but it is a critical one, especially for low-income African American families who face a myriad of obstacles to quality schooling for their children. They especially need supportive educators because often they did not have positive schooling experiences, lack resources and time to actively engage in their children's learning, and must deal with the stressors of being poor. The following unveils how Fairmont and Lincoln schools have defied pervasive negative perceptions that nothing "good" can arise from these and similar schools or the predominantly African American and low-income communities where they are based.

UNVEILING FAIRMONT ELEMENTARY SCHOOL AND THE COMMUNITY

African Americans moved into the area surrounding Fairmont Elementary School around 1952, but their children were not allowed to attend the school (Wright, 1994). Instead, they were bused to the all-Black schools throughout the city. African American students first enrolled in Fairmont Elementary School in 1956, 2 years after the passage of *Brown*. Over the next few years, White residents from the community (and other parts of the city) migrated rapidly to the surrounding suburbs, and the school became all Black within a few years. By the late 1960s and early 1970s, all the schools and communities in the northern section of the city were predominantly Black.

Fairmont was located in a low-income to working-class neighborhood on the north side of the city. One would immediately notice a scenic shift when approaching the school from a major road and, depending on the block, might see boarded-up houses or well-kept ones with yards as well maintained as any in St. Louis. Parts of the community showed signs of neglect; adjacent to the school, however, the homes were occupied and the yards litter-free. The evening news often highlighted crimes in this and similar communities in St. Louis rather than representing the everyday experiences of many of the residents. The media particularly focused on the wave of homicides linked to the selling of crack-cocaine that engulfed St. Louis and many other urban areas during the 1990s.

A sign that read "Welcome to Fairmont Elementary School" greeted parents and visitors inside the front entrance to the school. The shiny hardwood floors and the immaculate hallways defied stereotypic perceptions of an "inner-city" school. On the walls hung myriad honors, including *St. Louis Post-Dispatch* newspaper articles praising the school; photographs of prominent individuals who had once attended Fairmont; and baby photographs of students, faculty, and staff. Each of the 22 classrooms had a mailbox inscribed with the names and birthplaces of local and historical African American personalities, including Madame C. J. Walker, Jackie Joyner-Kersee, Benjamin Banneker, and Frederick Douglass.

Peering out the windows from the second floor of the school, one can gain a panoramic view of the parking lot and the side of the neighborhood opposite the playground. Almost every day on the playground, children would play Double-Dutch jump rope, basketball, and tumble. On one particular day, a group of African American female students engaged in a game in which each stepped out in front to lead a sequence of call and response. Mrs. Jackson, a teacher, observed and then smiled after each student finished her introduction. As soon as the whistle blew to end recess, a crossing-guard captain (an older student) ensured that the younger students proceeded in an orderly manner into the school. The school's newspaper, the *Fairmont Times*, allowed the students to display their journalistic talents (the school's academic emphasis was oral and written communication) and enabled teachers to communicate with parents.

With the exception of perhaps one or two White students during any given academic year, all of the approximately 370 students in prekindergarten through fifth grade were African American. Ninety-five percent qualified for free or reduced-price meals, and the school received Title I funds because of the high percentage of low-income students. The family composition was diverse, and many of the parents or guardians worked at blue-collar jobs (see Table 5.3). More than 27 percent of the families in the community lived below the poverty level (U.S. Census Bureau, 2000).

The predominantly African American faculty of about 40, which included two White teachers, was a stable force in the school and the community. As Table 5.4 illustrates, four of the African American teachers had taught for 30 years or more; two had taught for more than 40 years. Most received their certification to teach from Stowe, a formerly all-Black teachers college, or Harris–Stowe, a merger of Stowe with a historically all-White teachers college.

Although children within Fairmont's attendance zone had the option of participating in the desegregation plan, few parents exercised that option; instead, they chose Fairmont and were satisfied with the quality of education their children received there. Only ten families from the community sent their children to schools other than Fairmont; of those, seven families chose magnet schools in the city and three chose the predominantly White county schools. This finding was also confirmed by survey data of the school. Goldring and Smrekar (1995) found that 78.6 percent of the African American parents surveyed from Fairmont stated that the

Table 5.3. Fairmont family profiles, selected African American students.

FAMILY	FAIRMONT AFFILIATION	OCCUPATION	EDUCATION	YEARS IN COMMUNITY
Freeman: Married parents; three children	Neither parent attended Fairmont.	Ms. Freeman: Grocery clerk Mr. Freeman: Maintenance person	Ms. Freeman: Completed high school Mr. Freeman: Completed high school	11
Greene: Married parents; three children	Mr. and Mrs. Greene both attended Fairmont.	Mrs. Greene: Works in a pharmacy warehouse Mr. Greene: Supervisor at a plant	Mrs. Greene: Currently attends a community college Mr. Greene: Graduated from a four-year historically Black college	35
McHenry: Single mother; three children	None.	Unemployed	Less than high school degree	2
Moore: Married parents; four children	Mr. Moore attended Fairmont.	Mr. Moore: Construction Mrs. Moore: student at community college	Mr. Moore: High school Mrs. Moore: High school	10
Pinson: Married parents; four children	Mr. Pinson attended Fairmont.	Mr. Pinson: Truck driver	Mr. Pinson: High school and technical school	25
Roseman: Divorced mother; three children	Ms. Roseman attended Fairmont.	Forklift operator and custodian	Completed high school	23
Williams: Divorced mother, three children	Volunteer in school for 30 years.	Cook in a school cafeteria	Completed high school	30
Wooden: Grandparents raising five grandchildren	None.	Mr. Wooden: Retired from military	Both grandparents completed high school	42

Table 5.4. Fairmont educator profiles, selected faculty.

EDUCATOR	ETHNICITY	POSITION	YEARS AT SCHOOL	COMMUNITY AFFILIATION	EDUCATION	2001 STATUS
Ms. Burroughs	African American	First-grade teacher	Began teaching girls physical education at Fairmont in 1957	Once lived in the community, but moved away in 1982	Historically Black state college; Master's degree	Retired in 2000
Ms. Cain	African American	Instructional coordinator	Educator at the school for the past 32 years	Grew up in St. Louis	Historically Black state college; Master's degree	In 39th year at Fairmont
Mrs. Hall	African American	Title 1 teacher and coordinator	Began teaching at Fairmont in 1961	Grew up in Tennessee	Historically Black state university; Master's degree	Currently at the school and in her 41st year
Mrs. Hill	African American	Third-grade teacher	Taught for 37 years and had been a teacher at Fairmont since 1960	Attended schools near the community; mother lived in the community	Historically Black state college	Retired in 1997
Mrs. Jackson	African American	Fifth-grade teacher	Began teaching in 1970, and started working at Fairmont in 1989	Moved into a house across the street from Fairmont in 1982	Historically Black state college; Master's degree	12th year as a fifth-grade teacher in the school
Mrs. Linda	White	Third-grade teacher	Taught for 27 years in predominantly Black schools; 19 years at Fairmont	Grew up in St. Louis	Predominantly White state university; Master's degree	Left the school to pursue doctorate
Mrs. Lock	African American	Secretary	6 years	Children attended the school	Completed two-year college degree	Left the school in 1997
Mr. Miles	African American	Fourth-grade teacher	13 years	Moved into the community in 1981	Historically Black state college	20 years at Fairmont
Mrs. Raymond	African American	First-grade teacher	First-year teacher	Grew up in St. Louis	Predominantly White state university	Left the school in 1996
Mr. Steele	African American	Principal	Became principal of the school in 1972	Grew up in St. Louis	Historically Black state college; Master's degree	Principal for the past 29 years

school was their first choice, while 21.4 percent indicated that the school was their second choice. Ninety percent of the parents stated that they were satisfied in the choice of Fairmont as their child's school; 60 percent gave the school a grade of A and 30 percent gave the school a grade of B.

UNVEILING LINCOLN ELEMENTARY SCHOOL AND THE COMMUNITY

Lincoln Elementary School in Atlanta was a predominantly White school up to the 1950s. By the early 1960s, the school had become predominantly Black and was 675 students over capacity. Rather than allow Black students to attend the nearby all-White school, which was 750 students below capacity, White public school district administrators permitted mobile units at Lincoln and placed Black students on public transportation to travel to the school (Bayor, 1996). From the mid-1990s onward, the neighborhood surrounding Lincoln Elementary School underwent major demographic transitions.

Family profiles revealed a mixture of working-class Black families alongside families that lived below the poverty level. Sections of the community were becoming gentrified. Middle-class residents (primarily White, and many without children) purchased, restored, and upgraded some of the homes. Census data revealed that the poverty rate in this area—which comprised two census tracts—ranged from 37 to 47 percent.[5] Other areas in the community, as close as three blocks from the school, spoke to the level of poverty among some of the residents—directly contrasting with Atlanta's popular image as the Black Mecca.

In these other areas, it was not unusual to see groups of African American males and females between the ages of 15 and 25 hanging around corners and strolling the streets. Each day, a small number of African American males gathered at the "four way"—a common meeting place at a street corner—in search of a "hustle." Due to the influx of crack-cocaine into urban centers like Atlanta and the depressed economic situation for many low-income African Americans, some of these young people resorted to drugs and prostitution. In his ethnographic research of Black life in Philadelphia, the sociologist Elijah Anderson (1999) deftly describes the day-to-day experiences of Black males, such as the ones who hang near Lincoln Elementary School, and the reasons why many resort to participating in underground economic activities such as selling drugs. Unfortunately, elementary school children witnessed some of these sites on their way to school.

Near the side entrance to Lincoln, parents and relatives could be seen dropping off and picking up children before and after school. A multitude of vans would pick up some children and take them to after-school programs, while crossing guards, the principal, instructional coordinator, and teachers assisted students in crossing the streets on their way home. Across the street from the school, groups of children would visit a candy and snack store to purchase pickles, Now or Laters, potato chips, Red Hots, and sodas. It was a very small building that to the first-time visitor appeared vacant. Next to this store was a row of refurbished buildings, home to the Lincoln Community Program—a joint effort by the Atlanta public schools and a local university's pediatric program.

A K–5 school, Lincoln Elementary, greeted visitors with prints by African American artists near the school's entrance. Henry Ossawa Tanner's *Banjo Lesson* is prominently framed on a corridor's walls. A trophy case adorned the entrance and included letters from Georgia's secretary of state and a senator recognizing Lincoln as a "Georgia School of Excellence." Several trophies were from the school's corporate partner, a hotel chain in the city. The school's motto, mission statement, philosophy, and objectives for the year hung on the walls. Each morning, students proceeded in an orderly manner down the hall, greeting teachers and guests with "Bonjour." French was Lincoln's curricular focus, and the French teachers included an African American and two African teachers. Both of the African teachers were from African countries where French is the official language (Senegal and the Ivory Coast).

The student population of the Atlanta public schools at the time was more than 90 percent African American, although there has been a decrease in the overall African American student population in the system. Lincoln enrolled 561 students on average during the 2000–2001 academic year; 99 percent of these students were African American, and 94 percent of the students qualified for free or reduced-price meals. The Lincoln parents worked primarily at blue-collar jobs; some received public assistance (see Table 5.5). Of the more than 40 faculty members, 34 were African American; 3 were White, and 4 identified themselves as "Black and foreign-born" (they were from Ivory Coast, Jamaica, Nigeria, and Senegal).[6] (See Table 5.6.) The school featured a community program that included a school-based clinic, dental clinic, family resource center, child-care center, prekindergarten program, and family learning center.

TESTIMONIES

The following testimonies by the parents and the educators at Fairmont and Lincoln illustrate how the adults recognized the racial and social-class inequalities facing them and their children/students, but they did not allow

Table 5.5. Lincoln family profiles, selected students.

FAMILY	ETHNICITY	LINCOLN AFFILIATION	OCCUPATION	EDUCATION	YEARS IN COMMUNITY
Mrs. Anderson: Separated; grandmother. Ms. Aretha: Single; two children	African American	Mrs. Anderson attended Lincoln in 1959. Her children and grandchildren attended Lincoln.	Mrs. Anderson: Not employed. Ms. Aretha: Worked for a major hotel chain.	Mrs. Anderson completed some high school. Ms. Aretha completed high school.	Since the late 1950s
Barns: Single mother; three children	African American	Did not attend Lincoln.	Received federal assistance and disability.	Completed tenth grade.	21 years
A. Jones: Single mother; two children	African American	Did not attend Lincoln.	Received federal assistance.	Attended school up to twelfth grade.	18 years
T. Jones: Single mother; five children	African American	Attended Lincoln.	Received federal assistance.	Attended school up to eleventh grade.	26 years
Quinn: Married parents; two children	Guyanese	Mr. Quinn worked with the community program as a computer specialist.	Mr. Quinn: Computer specialist.	Mr. Quinn completed 2 years of college and is self-educated in computer technology.	13 years (born in Guyana)
Shields: Single mother; one child	African American	Did not attend Lincoln; PTA board member.	Staff person at Centers for Disease Control.	Some college.	5 years
Thomas: Divorced mother; four children	African American	All four children attended Lincoln.	Cashier for Atlanta Public Schools.	Completed eleventh grade; obtained G.E.D. and earned associate degree.	6 years
Tolliver: Separated mother; two children	African American	Former president and vice-president of PTA.	Provider of day care for people in community.	High school education.	8 years
Wright: Married parents; two children	African American	Mrs. Wright was PTA president.	Mrs. Wright owns a home cleaning business.	Completed high school; some college.	33 years

Table 5.6. Lincoln educator profiles, selected faculty.

EDUCATOR	ETHNICITY	POSITION	YEARS AT SCHOOL	COMMUNITY AFFILIATION	EDUCATION	2002 STATUS
Ms. Bond	African American	Reading curriculum teacher	33 years	Born in Atlanta	Historically Black private university; Master's degree	Reading curriculum teacher at Lincoln
Mrs. Bray	African American	Kindergarten teacher; taught third and fourth grades in early years	16 years	None	Historically Black private university; Bachelor's degree	Kindergarten teacher at Lincoln
Mrs. Brighton	White	Third-grade teacher	17 years at Lincoln; 35 years' teaching experience	Born outside Georgia	Predominantly White state university; Master's degree	Third-grade teacher at Lincoln
Mr. Cloud	African American	Fourth-grade teacher	5 years	None	Historically Black private university; Bachelor's degree	Left the school
Ms. Edwards	African American	Instructional coordinator	5 years	Moved from southeastern Georgia	Historically Black private university; Master's degree	Still at Lincoln in the same position
Mr. House	African American	Fourth-grade teacher	5 years as teacher; had student-taught at the school before being hired as a teacher	None; grew up in a northern city	Historically Black private university; Bachelor's degree	Left the school to start a business
Mrs. Jones	African American	Principal	1 year at Lincoln; 3 years' experience as an administrator; 23 years' experience as an educator	None; moved from southeastern Georgia	Historically Black state university and predominantly White state university; Master's degree	Still the principal at Lincoln
Mrs. Martin	African American	Retired paraprofessional	10 years	Born in Atlanta	Graduated from high school; some college completed	Retired
Ms. Murphy	African American	First-grade teacher	30 years as an educator at Lincoln	Born in Atlanta and grew up in a housing project	Historically Black private university; Master's degree	Passed away in fall 2000
Dr. Obasi	Nigerian	School counselor	2 years	Born in Nigeria	Historically Black private university; doctorate	Guidance counselor at Lincoln
Mrs. Vince	African American	Second-grade teacher	7 years	Grew up in the community; had left 20 years before time of the study	Historically Black private university; Bachelor's degree	Second-grade teacher at Lincoln

these forces to undermine their commitment to educate the children. These testimonies highlight (1) the intergenerational bonding between educators and families, (2) how the educators reached out to the community by welcoming the families into the schools, and (3) how the teachers in both schools affirmed the social and cultural experiences of the students through their interaction with the students and their families. Finally, the school leaders were intellectual and instructional leaders and functioned as a bridge between the schools and the larger communities where the schools were located. Furthermore, Fairmont and Lincoln served as "pillars" of their respective communities.

Intergenerational Bonding

Today, many educators who teach low-income African American children are disconnected—culturally, psychologically, and proximally—from the children they teach as well as from the communities where these children live. Consequently, these educators do not fully understand low-income African American children's experiences beyond the school. Fairmont's and Lincoln's connectedness to students, families, and their respective communities are worth noting.

For more than four decades, school personnel in both schools have had to find creative ways to build and sustain relationships with families and community residents. This was facilitated more easily in some instances than in others. In particular, some of the teachers at Fairmont lived in the community, had once lived there, or had relatives who lived there, reminiscent of the time when Black educators lived in the community where the school was located, attended its churches, and participated in its civic associations (Foster, 1997; Jones, 1981; Siddle Walker, 1996, 2000). For instance, Mr. Miles, a teacher, lived three blocks from Fairmont, was a referee at the local boys club, and taught Black history classes in the evenings at the neighborhood middle school.

To further illustrate the connections between the educators and the families, Mrs. Jackson, a teacher, and her husband had refurbished and moved into a house (across the street from the school) that had once belonged to his parents. The majority of the Fairmont educators were born in St. Louis, and some lived on the northern side of the city, where Black people overwhelmingly reside. Several knew the students' parents and grandparents on a personal basis. For instance, Mr. and Mrs. Wooden, the guardians of their five grandchildren and one of the first African American families to move into the Fairmont community in 1957, were close friends with Ms. Burroughs, a teacher at the school.

At both Fairmont and Lincoln, at least three generations of some African American families had attended the school. This intergenerational bonding was exemplified by grandparents at Lincoln such as Ms. Anderson, and by Ms. Williams, a parent at Fairmont who continued to enroll her youngest child in the school even after moving out of the attendance zone and into an outlying county. According to Mr. Steele, the principal of Fairmont, the continuity of generations of family members who attended Fairmont reflected parents' confidence that the school would provide the best education for their children:

> The parents that once attended Fairmont as students have a certain allegiance and an appreciation for the school. They know that they received a quality education. So, in turn, they want their children to come here. The parents at Fairmont enjoyed their experiences while attending Fairmont; therefore, they want their children to have the same kind of experiences. Sometimes they would come from various parts of the city to bring them back to where they had received a good education.

Ms. Anderson, a grandparent at Lincoln who had once attended the school, described the nature of the bonding between Lincoln and African American families:

> Lincoln Elementary School has a good reputation. It's the reason I went, my children went, my grandkids went, and the grandchildren of my grandchildren will be going. I always tried to keep them [the children and grandchildren] in Lincoln because they had everything that they needed to learn. They just had everything.

These schools' deep connections with African American families, however, would experience new challenges during the 1990s. How would these schools continue the intergenerational bonding given the changes within the schools and the communities? Although Fairmont was relatively stable in terms of student population, its faculty was becoming older. In the future, school personnel would have to find ways to ensure that the next generation of educators personified the commitment displayed by those who were currently there. Lincoln, on the other hand, had already undergone a major transition in its faculty. In addition, the community surrounding Lincoln was experiencing a demographic shift that could have dire implications for the school.

Building Trust: Reaching Out and Welcoming In

The Fairmont and Lincoln educators did not wait for parents to initiate participation; they reached out and welcomed these parents into the school. School personnel at Fairmont made special efforts to accommodate parents' unique situations. As one teacher noted, "There have been instances in which a parent expressed that she could not read, and I allowed the parent to monitor the students instead of reading to them." At the annual Meet-the-Teacher Night, the staff and faculty agreed to change the starting time of the program from 5:00 P.M. to 7:30 P.M. to enable a larger number of parents to attend. Consequently, there was standing room only as over 200 parents lined the walls and covered the floor of the gymnasium. In addition, the school rewarded students with a pizza or popcorn party for the homerooms with the most parents in attendance at school functions. According to Mr. Steele, the principal, "A lot of the students let their parents know that their class could receive a party if their parents attended a meeting or a function." Ms. Linda, a White teacher who had taught at Fairmont for 19 years, affirmed Mr. Steele's statement:

> Mr. Steele, the principal, would have roller-skating parties or something like that for the children if they told their parents to attend events at the school. Once parents come into the school, teachers have to get them to a comfort level. As a school, you want to give the students and the parents something. The main thing that you want to do is to make that connection with the parents, the child, and the school.

Lincoln Elementary had a similar history of supporting parental involvement. Mrs. Martin, a recently retired paraprofessional who had worked at Lincoln for 10 years, described the involvement of parents at that school:

> We had this one parent. She had a disability problem, but she could function. That parent came up, she came up about 2 or 3 years, and I'll never forget! She would come in and tell the children stories. And that teacher would find her something to do. And the children got used to it. Her [the parent's] daughter was in that room, and her daughter was very proud that her mama could come up and do something. Because she was very protective, she was just a kindergarten child. I'll never forget it. She was protective of her mother because she knew that she was smarter than her mother. But after her mother came up, and the teacher let her

come up and tell stories to the children, that child was real proud. And it's just the small things; that's what I'm saying. The small things that teachers need to do more of to bring parents in. Because parents, you have to be real with them. You don't come up with, "I know you can do this and I know you can do that." You find out what they can do and you work with that.

To further encourage interaction among parents and school personnel, Lincoln sponsored Ladies' Night Out and Men's Night Out. At Ladies' Night Out, male teachers and the students' male relatives prepared meals for the female parents and teachers. Likewise, as the following field notes illustrate, Men's Night Out included a home-cooked meal:

In the kitchen some female teachers were trying to ensure that the evening went well. Ms. Christopher, one of the most visible staff members in the school, who often assumes responsibility for coordinating the teacher and staff annual holiday breakfast, was in the kitchen giving orders. I had been away from the school for about a month [because of a family illness] and some of the teachers asked where had I been and told me they were glad to see me. . . . Each adult male sponsored a male child during the evening. There were about 50 adult males and about 100 or more children at the evening event. Mrs. Jones, the principal, was wearing her apron and had also been busy cooking for the evening. . . . Mr. Gooden, the assistant principal, was sharp as a tack—with his slacks, sport coat, and shined shoes. He always dressed well so as to model professionalism to the other teachers as well as the students. Joe Hamilton, the [African American] quarterback at Georgia Tech Institute of Technology, was the keynote speaker.

The educators were not without challenges in their efforts to involve parents. Educators in both schools noted that extra efforts were made to encourage parental participation. They also observed that the schools could not rely primarily on attendance at PTA meetings as an indicator of parents' interest in their children's schooling. For example, during the 1999–2000 academic year, PTA meetings at Lincoln were not attended at the level that Mrs. Wright, a parent and the school's PTA president, had hoped. As the year progressed, attendance dropped from 75 parents and children to about 50 parents and children in the latter part of the academic year. One parent felt that the 6:00 P.M. meeting time was one of the reasons for the lower turnout. Nevertheless, families turned out in large numbers for other school functions such as Ladies' Night Out and the Black History Month program.

In their historical case studies of African American parents' relationships with their children's schools, Jones (1981) and Siddle Walker (1996) noted that Black parents did not actively participate in the day-to-day school activities or decision making. Instead, parents and other people in the community supported school personnel by offering assistance—for example, contributing school supplies and volunteering when requested or during special events such as PTA meetings. Black families *trusted* that Black educators would act in the best interest of their children because many of the teachers were their neighbors or members of their church. Unfortunately, today many low-income African American parents are labeled as uninvolved and uninterested parents if they do not regularly attend school functions. Furthermore, because of some parents' lack of schooling or their discomfort with the middle-class settings of schools, they are reluctant to visit their children's schools (Edwards, 1996; Epstein, 1986). Mr. Miles, a teacher at Fairmont, provided a wonderful example of how a sense of trust prevented a possible altercation and mitigated the class boundaries so common between teachers and low-income families today.

> A couple of years ago, a couple of parents came up [to the school]; they were kind of upset at a situation at the school, and I knew the parents. So I talked to the mother and explained things to her. . . . She said, "Okay, Mr. Miles, I understand what you mean." So I feel that communication is very important. A lot of times, parents may have this feeling that we, as educators, feel that we have the attitude that we are better than they are. I tell them, "I am no better than you are; we just have different jobs."

Ms. Aretha, a Lincoln parent, recounted the trust between her and her daughter's kindergarten teacher, Ms. Eileen:

> Like Ms. Eileen, the kindergarten teacher. Over the summer she knew that I was working like weird hours. . . . Two months or a month before school started or so, she [the daughter] went to stay with Ms. Eileen. She knew that my hours were crazy. So that was good. That was great. She would say that Monique reminded her— my daughter's name is Shineka, but we call her Monique—but she always saying Monique reminded her of herself when she was a little girl.

How can schools create a trust so deep that low-income African American parents feel that the educators in the school really care about them and understand their situation? Because of school and district policies, educators are prevented from engaging in the kind of interactions that Ms. Eileen had with Ms. Aretha and her daughter, Shineka. Many of these school districts' policies are intended to limit the possibility of inappropriate relations between teachers and students, which has been a highly publicized concern in recent years. However, Ms. Eileen had gotten to know Ms. Aretha beyond the traditional teacher–parent relationship; their bond of trust reassured Ms. Aretha that she, too, was committed to Shineka's well-being.

On the other hand, Mr. Miles at Fairmont was able to resolve the possible altercation with a parent because of his deep commitment to the families and the children as well as his identification with the community; he lived there. The depth of caring by Ms. Eileen toward Ms. Aretha's daughter exemplified what Cornell West (1988) terms a "love ethic" for Black children and what Jim Scheurich (1998) also described in his research on schools that cared about and were successful with low-income children of color. Like other effective teachers of low-income African American children, the educators at Fairmont and Lincoln saw themselves as having life experiences similar to those of the children they taught (Irvine, 1999a, 1999b; Stanford, 1997); they took on the role of "othermothers" (Hill-Collins, 2000; Irvine, 1999a) and strongly identified with the communities where they taught (Casey, 1993; Foster, 1995; Ladson-Billings, 1994).

Cultural Affirmation and Consciousness Raising

Although varied, the nature of the cultural affirmation in the schools was evident in the atmosphere within each school (e.g., the assembly programs, hallway displays, and even some teachers' attire) rather than explicitly in the curriculum. There were obvious similarities between many of the educators and their students in racial and ethnic identity. Although sharing a racial or ethnic identity with students does not automatically mean that one is committed to their welfare, the educators at these schools expressly wanted to teach low-income African American students (Gay, 1997).

School personnel at both schools enthusiastically took part in African Americans' historical and cultural celebrations. Every year, Lincoln Elementary displayed the traveling Black History Museum—a collection of significant inventions by African Americans during the 19th and 20th centuries. At Fairmont Elementary, the Black History Month program was filled with the story of Africans' experiences prior to enslavement as well as in America, as captured in the field notes on the program.

The theme of the program is "Portraits in Black and White."
African and African American symbols hang on the walls. The

children proceed into the auditorium to the tune of Kirk Franklin and Family's "Why We Sing." A little girl comes on stage and says, "It all started back in Africa, thousands of years before Jesus Christ. Later, slavery deprived us as Black people of our language, culture, and religion." Soon afterwards, a choir of young children begins singing "Kumbaya, My Lord" and "Joshua Fought the Battle of Jericho." The choir takes the audience on a chronological musical journey, beginning with African and African American spirituals and moving up to R&B music. Songs include "Go Down Moses," "Traveling, Trying to Make Heaven My Home," "Down and Out," "I Got the Blues," "They Call It Stormy Monday," "His Eye Is on the Sparrow," "Respect," sung by Aretha Franklin, "Billy Jean" by Michael Jackson, and "The Greatest Love of All," recorded by Whitney Houston. Students are reciting poems by Langston Hughes and Maya Angelou. Throughout the singing and reading of poetry, students dramatize the lives of African American heroes and heroines and important events in Black history.

The ambience in each school and the educators' pedagogical and interaction styles created an environment in which African American children could see themselves and their culture within the schooling process (Honora, 2003). The ambience and the interaction styles began to inform the students' critical understanding of their historical and cultural heritage—a process that King (1991) described as "emancipatory pedagogy," Ladson-Billings (1994) called "culturally relevant" teaching, and Lynn (1999) called "critical race pedagogy." The educators used their cultural capital—in this case, their knowledge of African American history and culture—to begin to shape the children's critical understanding of their history. Their ways of conveying that understanding differed in the two schools. Fairmont educators reminded the students of the nearly insurmountable odds that Black people had overcome. A fifth-grade female student exemplified this focus in her narration of the Black History Month program:

> The spirituals and singing enabled us as African Americans to make it through the hard times. Our singing carried our emotions. As Black people, we were resilient and survived the horrors of slavery, discrimination, racism, and prejudice.

On the other hand, it was not out of the ordinary to see educators at Lincoln wearing African garb or clothing accented with Kente cloth patterns. Lincoln educators made connections with an African past through assembly programs and by displaying classroom projects in the school's hallways, such as maps of the African continent, vegetables with African origins (e.g., okra), and African masks. Although subtle, such efforts explicitly connected the African American students with Africa and their cultural and historical heritage (Morris, 2003). Educators in both schools ensured that Black children learned about their cultural and historical heritage. The different ways of doing so in the two schools were partly a manifestation of the generational differences between the educators in the two schools and partly reflective of the cosmopolitan nature of Atlanta in comparison with St. Louis. Lincoln's educators were younger, and, although nearly all of them were Black, they represented diverse Black cultural experiences.

Moreover, the educators made classroom lessons relevant to the students' everyday experiences (Boykin, 1994; Ladson-Billings, 1994; Lee, 1993, 1995; Scheurich, 1998). For example, Ms. Blackmon, a fifth-grade teacher at Lincoln, tried almost in vain to get her students to comprehend the adage, "An apple doesn't fall too far from the tree." To make the point, she used the example of a teacher in the school whose mother had also been a teacher, but to no avail. Afterwards, Ms. Blackmon decided to use the students' cultural capital by providing them with an example from hip-hop culture, a potentially powerful tool for teaching literacy to urban and African American students (Morrell & Duncan-Andrade, 2002). For many of these young people, hip-hop culture, particularly rap music, played an essential role in shaping their identity and their understanding of society. Ms. Blackmon asked the students if they knew Master P, the rapper and executive of No Limit Records. Once the students indicated that they had heard of Master P, she then asked if they knew the name of Master P's son. In a concerted manner, the students exclaimed, "Lil' Romeo!" As Master P's son, Lil' Romeo had followed in his father's footsteps by also becoming a rapper. Thus he was not far from his roots.

Classroom teaching at both schools emphasized skill generation. This was spurred, in part, by the accountability movement, which placed a heavy emphasis on standardized tests as measures of effective schooling. Yet for years before that movement gained momentum, Mr. Steele's faculty had prepared the children for the state's standardized tests. Likewise, Mrs. Jones, in her monthly newsletter to school personnel and parents, regularly informed the Lincoln community of the importance of the children's preparing for and performing well on these high-stakes tests. Scheurich (1998) also noted how the principals and teachers in the schools that he studied thoroughly prepared their children for standardized tests, to show that their schools were equal to other schools. The educators at Fairmont and Lincoln knew that they, too, were being "watched by others," who equated low performance on a test with presumed African American intellectual inferiority.

Test results were annually published in the *Atlanta Journal Constitution* and the *St. Louis Post-Dispatch* and compared with those of nearby school districts, many of which had majority-White student populations. The publishing of the schools' test results—without noting the deep-rooted structural and historical inequalities between the experiences of students enrolled in the majority-Black, low-income public school districts in St. Louis and Atlanta, and those enrolled in predominantly White, middle-class suburban school districts—reinforced negative perceptions of African American people and their intellect. Consequently, the African American principals at both schools constantly protected their faculty and students' dignity against these subtle attacks (Benham, 1997; Dillard, 1995, 2000) by making sure that Fairmont and Lincoln were among the best-performing schools on statewide standardized tests. They preached to the faculty and the students the importance of working "twice as hard" in preparing for the tests, even though the tests did not always measure the actual learning that occurred in the schools.

BRIDGING WORLDS AND SAVING HOPE

A major issue facing many urban schools today is the high degree of teacher turnover, which disrupts the stability of the school as well as the instructional process (Darling-Hammond, Wise, & Klein, 1995; Ingersoll, 2002). Teacher stability in any school is important, but especially in schools that serve primarily low-income and minority students. Usually, the vast majority of teachers in such schools are new to the field and lack the experience necessary to develop a repertoire of skills and strategies for addressing student needs, a circumstance that can adversely affect student learning (Darling-Hammond et al., 1995; National Center for Education Statistics, 2003). The mean total of teaching experience among teachers at Fairmont School was 19.4 years, whereas the mean for all other neighborhood schools in St. Louis was 6.2 years. Fairmont had the highest teacher stability rate of all the elementary schools in St. Louis. Its stability was impressive, considering the high faculty turnover in many schools in urban communities.

On the other hand, the mean total of teaching experience among the teachers at Lincoln during the 1997–1998 academic year was 13.0 years, as compared with the school system's mean of 14.8 years. Lincoln's mean dropped further when some of the teachers who had been at the school for an extended period retired at the end of the 1998–1999 academic year.

The school hired more than 20 new teachers over the course of 2 years (1999–2001). As the new principal, Mrs. Jones recognized that she needed not only to secure the confidence of the community but also to build a "sense of community" among her almost entirely new faculty and staff: "I decided to bring in some new teachers I had a part in selecting. I believe that you have to have people who embrace the same philosophy that you embrace in order to make a school work."

Senior teachers at both schools set an example for the expectations regarding students' academic performance, collegiality among the faculty and staff, and connections with the families and the community. Ms. Cain, who was in her 39th year at Fairmont during 2000–2001, was one such example. Initially a classroom teacher and later an instructional coordinator, Ms. Cain played an integral role in defining and shaping the Fairmont community. Mrs. Bond and Ms. Murphy, teachers for 33 and 30 years, respectively, did likewise at Lincoln. As indicated by the following parents, these teachers were major reasons why they chose to send their children to the schools:

> If I had to do it all over again, I would send my child back to Fairmont because they have some of the same teachers that were there when I attended the school. (Mr. Greene, father of a Fairmont student)

> I would say, last year when we had a lot of the older teachers that are there, we had Ms. Murphy that would really go out her way to know where you lived and really got involved with your family if you needed something. Ms. Murphy really went out to make sure that the school was connected with the families and the community. (Ms. Barns, mother of a Lincoln student)

The character of a school is not fixed in time. Abrupt changes and teacher turnover can instantly change the relationship between a school and its community. In the present era of school accountability and No Child Left Behind (NCLB), school districts are moving principals who have shown success in one school to schools where they want the principal to produce similar results. And when principals leave, so do their faculty and staff, who often try to relocate where the principal has gone. Principal and teacher tenure are particularly important for schools that serve low-income Black children: children who are already on the margins and face numerous instabilities in their lives. In the case of Lincoln Elementary, Dr. Frazier's unexpected passing in 1999 created a critical period of adjustment in which many of the teachers were uncertain about the prospects of a new principal. Rather than come under a new administration, some retired or transferred.

Fairmont Elementary, on the other hand, managed the abrupt but temporary loss of its principal, Mr. Steele, in the best way that it knew how. In the spring of 1994, Mr. Steele accepted a job in the central office of the St. Louis public school system. A new principal came on board. The combined impact of Mr. Steele's departure and the new principal's arrival caused temporary instability in the school. According to one teacher, "She [the new principal] arrived with a totally different leadership style. After a few weeks, some of the teachers wanted transfers; even those who had been here for some time considered early retirement." Within a month after Mr. Steele's departure, some teachers and parents contacted him and asked if he would consider returning. After another month, Mr. Steele returned to Fairmont, saying, "I couldn't stay away for too long from Fairmont. From the way I heard it, nothing was going right at the school. So I thought about it and talked with the teachers and decided to go back home to Fairmont."

As principal at Fairmont for 29 years, Mr. Steele had been an integral part in the success of the school. He involved himself and his family in the affairs of the school and attended weddings, graduations, and funerals in the community. According to one teacher, "Mr. Steele is an administrator who will do whatever is necessary to help ensure the success of the children at Fairmont. Everything revolves around the children."

Likewise, Lincoln Elementary built a reputation for meeting the schooling and social needs of the students because of the efforts by the former principal, Dr. Frazier, who had set high standards for teachers and students and garnered resources to assist the teachers and students in the overall teaching and learning processes. Mr. House, a fourth-grade teacher, described Dr. Frazier's expectations:

> Dr. Frazier had a reputation for being a very stern principal. Being a very no-holds-barred principal when it came to doing what's best for the children. . . . She was a six-thirty- [in the morning] to-seven-o'clock-in-the-evening principal. It was nothing for her to put in more than 12 hours a day. So, with all of this coming at you, and you know, you're 23, 24 years old, of course you're going to come in and work hard. But at the same time, all of these veterans are telling you, "If you come here you're going to work and going to work hard, and you're working with at-risk children." . . . But what's expected is the same from you as a teacher with exceptionally bright students.

Mrs. Jones spoke of the expectations of her as the new principal and how people would often remind her of Dr. Frazier's legacy at Lincoln:

> Well, every single person that I have come into contact with has told me that, has told me unequivocally, "You have big shoes to fill." Dr. Frazier was this icon in the Lincoln community and, you know, that's great. I don't feel intimidated about her because one thing about people, you work within your time. . . . I have a time. I said that Dr. Frazier was at this school for 11 years. She's a product of Atlanta. The Atlanta public schools. I'm an outsider coming in. This is my first year as a principal. Dr. Frazier was 20 years my senior. . . . I can't be her. I'm not trying to fill her shoes. I have my own mission; I have my own time.

Mrs. Jones believed that as a teacher "you set the high expectations; you expect for [students] to learn. . . . I don't care where you were in Atlanta, Georgia—the most affluent school—give these children the same thing."

Like Black principals in the segregated South, Mr. Steele's and Dr. Frazier's roles extended beyond the boundaries of the school and continued an African American educational leadership tradition of bridging the internal world of the school with the larger community. Mr. Steele and Dr. Frazier played key roles in creating high expectations for staff and students, solidifying the school with the community (the neighborhood and citywide communities), and fostering collegiality among staff and faculty. Dr. Frazier and Mr. Steele realized that it was essential to garner support from individuals and agencies beyond the school in order to provide additional human and financial resources to their students (Henig et al., 1999). These leaders' concern for students and understanding of their communities are qualities shared by all principals who are effective in involving families in schools (Goldring & Rallis, 1993; Sebring & Bryk, 2000) and by all African American principals who successfully work with African American children and families (Lomotey, 1989). Their roles transcended the metaphor of a bridge. Like the African American urban school principals in studies by Dillard (1995) and Reitzug and Patterson (1998), Mr. Steele and Dr. Frazier cared deeply about low-income African American children and their future.

PILLARS OF STRENGTH

Historically, the Black church was the primary pillar of the Black community and offered stability and support to families and communities. It served as a place for social, cultural, marital, religious, spiritual, festive, and educational matters during slavery, during segregation, and afterwards (Lincoln & Mamiya, 1990). Black schools were second in importance to the Black church in influencing the lives of African Americans. Lincoln Elementary and Fairmont Elementary assumed the roles of "pillars" in their respective communities and were the centers for many community activities and events. One such activity that symbolically captured the significant role of the schools in their communities was the annual carnival, held in the fall at Lincoln and in the spring at Fairmont. For this event, school personnel invited parents and community residents to enjoy a day of games, activities, and refreshments. Parents looked forward to the event and helped to plan it. Furthermore, after-school child-care programs were based at the schools, and Fairmont and Lincoln offered tutorial assistance to parents studying for the GED (General Educational Development) diploma.

Urban schools and educators contend with numerous social issues that overshadow the teaching of content. A large number of students at Fairmont and Lincoln arrived at school in need of services beyond schooling. Throughout the schoolyear, Lincoln and the adjacent Lincoln Community Program maintained a supply of donated clothes for children who needed them. The Lincoln Community Program, created in 1995, assisted Lincoln school personnel in meeting the needs of families and children. According to the brochure at the front entrance to the program, the program's vision was to "ensure that every child in the Lincoln community is equipped with everything she or he needs to succeed in school." Fairmont also kept a supply of donated winter clothing for students who arrived at school without a coat or who did not have adequate clothing during the winter months.

The roles that these schools assumed in their respective communities were affected by educational and housing policies in each city, as well as by demographic shifts. Changes in social and educational policies had been precipitated by the changing nature of urban areas across the United States, areas characterized by a dwindling industrial presence, rampant unemployment, and governmental neglect (Wilson, 1996). The St. Louis desegregation plan was an opportunity for some African American parents to educate their children in schools perceived to be better than the predominantly Black schools in the city.

Lincoln Elementary School existed amid major urban revitalization in Atlanta, spawned by the city's preparation for and hosting of the 1996 Summer Olympics. Newcomers to Atlanta were seeking out affordable homes in the city. The community increasingly felt the impact of the demographic shift from a predominantly African American and low- and fixed-income residential population to a population of professionals, which included a growing number of White, single, and middle-class residents.

Many low- and fixed-income African Americans, particularly the elderly, were being forced to sell their homes because of increased taxes or their inability to fix up their homes (Holmes, 1998; Shelton, 2001). Families that rented found themselves priced out of the rental market. Mrs. Thomas, a Lincoln parent, recounted her mother's experience:

> My mom owned her own home, right, and that house been sitting there since before I was born. I went to pay my mama's taxes and my mom don't have no income or nothing like that, but I had to go pay her taxes. When I went down there to pay her taxes, this lady at the tax place said, "Well, it's good to pay your taxes because they come down here and look on the tax record and see who ain't paid their taxes and we just go and take their taxes."

Mrs. Brighton, a White teacher who has taught at Lincoln for the past 17 years, commented:

> We had a situation last year where there is an apartment complex that sits off on a hill on Heritage Drive, and they just all at once moved everybody out of these apartments. I have two children living there, and so now they have no homes—because the owner was going to renovate these apartments and sell them for garden houses, or something like that; I forget what they were calling them. And he was asking for $180,000 per unit. . . . Again, I had been there because I had two children living there in those apart-ments, and he did not take care of those apartments as rental property.

The community surrounding Lincoln, with its close proximity to down-town Atlanta and various centers of culture, was highly sought after. Mrs. Bond, a teacher for 33 years at Lincoln, summed up the consequences for Lincoln Elementary School and the community if this trend continued:

> I don't know if Lincoln will still be opened 10 years from now because we pull 90 percent of the children, they come from the East Avenue projects. Several of the children live in homes their grand-parents own. If the trend continues where single people move in, the numbers will go down. Older people are dying out. Some families will keep their houses. Whites are fixing up the homes.

Lincoln's student population declined as a result of housing shifts in this and similar Atlanta communities. For example, the school's population declined from 633 students in the 1998–1999 academic year to 485 students in the 2001–2002 academic year, a 23.4 percent loss. Although some White families moved into the community, they chose not to enroll their children in Lincoln, thereby avoiding the creation of a naturally integrated school. White parents refused to enroll their children in the local, predominantly Black schools (Hill, 2003). In one community, Whites represented more than 30 percent of the population but only 3 percent of the student population in the predominantly African American school that they were zoned to attend.

Between 2002 and 2006, parts of the area near Lincoln Elementary began to change beyond recognition. Two blocks away, on the main thoroughfare that borders the school and the community, recently sprouted shopping centers feature the familiar suburban mall-like stores such as Lowe's; Target; Bed, Bath, and Beyond; and Kroger's grocery store. White singles, couples, and families can be seen walking their dogs along the newly paved and neatly arranged streets or just sitting on the benches located in this carefully planned shopping center. Maybe this is what is meant by "urban revitalization." Whether Lincoln Elementary and its current students become beneficiaries or casualties of this gentrification remains to be seen. But one thing is definite, the population of African Americans in the community and school will continue to decline in this now-coveted area of the city.

In concluding this chapter, it is easier to identify problems that plague urban and predominantly African American schools and communities than to prescribe solutions. Research and policy studies that emphasize "the problem" with schools receive a great deal of attention and funding (Lightfoot, 1983) but foster a deficit approach to educational policy. Reforms and policies such as NCLB, charter schools, vouchers, and high-stakes testing have been supported in part by highlighting the despair in urban and predominantly African American schools in the United States.

Some may believe that it is irresponsible for scholars to highlight academically successful urban and predominantly African American schools, especially in a political climate that continues to ignore racial and social-class inequalities. In truth, however, it is the *failure* to study schools such as Fairmont and Lincoln—which have demonstrated success in the education of low-income African American students—that is irresponsible. The scholarly neglect of successful African American schools continues to foster one-dimensional representations of African American people and institutions. Historically, and as revealed in this chapter, African American people and institutions have had to adapt to larger structural forces, such as racism and class subordination, by providing cultural sustenance for themselves (Billingsley, 1968; Du Bois, 1935). For instance, over the past

40 years, personnel at both Fairmont and Lincoln took a previously all-White school and modified it so that it began to serve the needs of African American students, families, and communities—a testament to African Americans' "adaptive vitality" (Karenga, 1993).

Although Fairmont and Lincoln do not fit the pattern of schooling in most urban areas of the United States, what role might similarly situated schools play in educating low-income African American students? Might an emphasis on understanding these schools offer ways to improve the educational experiences of low-income Black students who continue to attend urban schools in the other Nazareths of the United States?[7]

CHAPTER 6

A Man Named Mr. Wooden: Generational Wisdom and the Care of Black Children

This chapter presents excerpts from many conversations and interviews with Mr. Wooden, a resident of the 'Ville who lived across the street from Fairmont Elementary School in St. Louis. Also highlighted are key themes from interviews with his granddaughter, Renee. When the study began in 1994, Renee was a fifth-grade student at Fairmont. During the fall of 2007, she was a graduate student in sociology at a university in Chicago. The interviews and conversations with Mr. Wooden and Renee are presented in a first-person narrative because of the longitudinal nature of the conversations, particularly with Mr. Wooden, over the years. This first-person narrative is similar to the kind conducted by scholars such as Anderson (1978, 1990, 1999), Shaw (1966), and Pattillo-McCoy (1999), who used narratives to capture the emotions and experiences of the participants in the study through their eyes.

For instance, through Mr. Wooden's first-person narrative, the reader becomes a witness to the change and continuity in the community over the past half-century, gains greater insight into the nature of Fairmont's connections with families and the community over time, and begins to understand the expectations that Mr. Wooden and his wife had for their children, grandchildren, and great-grandchildren. Consistent with the first-person narrative, the participants speak for themselves, thus keeping the author's editing to a minimal.

GETTING TO KNOW THE WOODEN FAMILY

The Wooden family of St. Louis is not the kind of urban Black family that the news media and even academics often portray. Yes, the grandparents have taken in grandchildren and raised them. However, this was not because the children's mother was a crack addict, as we are so used to reading and hearing about. James and Diane Wooden gained custody of their daughter Janice's six daughters (including Renee) when Janice died from a brain tumor in 1986.

Mr. and Mrs. Wooden later raised their granddaughter Rhonda's three children after Rhonda, who was blind, and her husband, who was partially blind, divorced. Rather than allow the state to place the children into foster care, Mr. and Mrs. Wooden took custody of the children in 1999.

Mr. and Mrs. Wooden thus raised three generations of children. When Mrs. Wooden became ill, Mr. Wooden became her caretaker. She passed during the spring of 2007. Mr. Wooden also helps take care of his mother, who is 97 years old and lives next door. That he has done so is remarkable, given that he has had multiple heart attacks. Each time he had a heart attack, the faculty and staff at Fairmont Elementary raised money to assist him in his recuperation.

For more than a decade, from 1994 through 2006, I have been a guest in the Wooden home to talk about the changes and continuity in the Fairmont community and school, the St. Louis desegregation plan, and the progress of his grandchildren. Always with a smile, Mr. Wooden, a light-brown African American man of about 5 feet and 7 inches, would greet me at his front door. For more than a decade since we first met, I made numerous sojourns back to St. Louis, partly to remain current with the field work and the research sites as well as to collect new data on the changes in the schools and communities.

The Wooden family's house is a brownstone in North St. Louis. I would describe the Wooden family as "everyday people" because drastic events do not frame their lives; instead, a multitude of smaller events have given character to how their lives become lived. I also describe the Wooden family as "everyday people" because they have had a constant presence (literally every day) in the Fairmont school and community for more than half a century.

Mr. Wooden and his family were part of the first wave of Black families to integrate the community and Fairmont Elementary School in the 1950s. Mr. Wooden witnessed White flight from the community and school during the early 1960s, the economic downturn in St. Louis during the 1970s, the influx of crack-cocaine in the 1980s, the departure of lower-middle-class Black families, and the gentrification that began to take place in the late 1990s. Yet he remains a pillar in the community. The family has lived in the same house since moving there in 1957. This is unique for any family, let alone African American families, in the urban centers of the United States. The Wooden family is not unlike the group of urban Black families that Elijah Anderson (1999) discusses—families whose lives reflect decency. The following captures Mr. Wooden's life experiences within the context of key themes presented in this book.

MR. WOODEN'S NARRATIVE

MY LIFE

I was born on January 15, 1929, the same day that Dr. Martin Luther King Jr. was born. I was born in Louisiana. Some of my family members lived in New Orleans. I lived with my aunt, who was my mother's sister, and my great-grandmother. My father was in the military, and he traveled all of the time. He finally got stationed in St. Louis and I came up here to live with my father and mother. But I had attended high school back in Louisiana and also went to Dillard University in New Orleans. I did not finish Dillard, but because I was still young, I just came up to St. Louis to live with my parents. Where my parents and I lived was only a couple of blocks from where Ms. Burroughs at Fairmont lived. She and I have been knowing each other for some time. We grew up about two blocks from each other. . . . So, since I moved to St. Louis to live with my parents, I enrolled at Stowe Teachers College. You know, back then the college was an all-Black school. It later became part of Harris Teachers College, the White school. So I was in college, and then they called me into the army in 1951. I was in Korea working with military personnel records. After I was re-leased and returned to the United States, I got a job here in St. Louis at the military personnel record center. I worked there for 33 years until I retired in 1986. All my work now is volunteer work. I volunteer with the North Side Community Center, with my church, with Fairmont School. I was a Scoutmaster for 26 years and had one of the best troops in the city!

I met my wife, who is from Mississippi, right here in St. Louis. We had one child, and I was also a foster parent. My daughter passed of a brain tumor, and I got six of her children. And I've had them, like, 6 years [then in 1994]. And I raised them. Put one through Jackson State University in Mississippi. She graduated last July [in 1993]. And I have one in college. She's going to profes-sional school. And two in high school here. And then there is Renee, who is across the street at Fairmont. And I have another granddaughter who is blind. The reason why I took the children in is because they are my blood. These are my daughter's children and I was not going to just let them be out there alone, or be in foster care. This is how my mother taught me, and that is why I do it. My mother is here, living right next door to me. But my wife's mother lived in Iowa, and a lot of her relatives live in Mississippi.

My relatives—when I had relatives—lived in Louisiana and New York. So we visit. We would go to see them, and they come to visit us.

CHANGE AND CONTINUITY IN THE COMMUNITY

Well, when we first moved here into this neighborhood, it was a mixed block. We had White and Black, or Black and White, whichever way you want to say it. And now it's all Black. All the Whites moved out. Back in the fifties, the neighborhood was mixed for a short time. All of these people who lived here were working-class people. So they all had jobs. They were not on any type of welfare or anything like that. Now, the community has changed since I have been here. . . . As a community, we still try to work together. Trying to keep out the riff-raff or drug dealers, or whatever you want to call them, and trying to pull together. For example, the people in the block have a unit where they meet, say, once a month. And they decide on what needs to be done to help their block, like beautification or trying to set up flowers or cutting the grass. . . . And there are other things. Right now they don't all come to mind, but there are a lot of things. And in the summertime, block units get together and order plants to set out, and they give them out to the different houses. If something is wrong, like the alley needs cleaning, or something like that, because some of the kids have a tendency, instead of throwing the garbage into the trash can, they will perhaps throw it by the trash can. Cleaning that up and seeing that the alleys are swept out and things like that; those are things that I try to do. If someone can't cut their grass, we will pull together and cut it for them. . . .

Now [in 2005], the community is changing even more. White people are coming in here quicker than you can imagine. A lot of White people are now moving into these areas here in North St. Louis. And the prices of the homes are going up every day. So there are a lot of changes going on in this community.

THE DESEGREGATION PLAN

I'm not interested in the county schools. I don't see why my children can't get the same education right here in the city of St. Louis that they could get in the county. Why do they have to do all of this traveling back and forth, losing time? It just doesn't make sense to me. I prefer having the school right here in the city. If they don't have what it takes, then with all of the teachers out there, they should be brought in to make it have what it takes. So I see no difference in this school and the county school. Maybe parents who send their children out there know something I don't know. But I know about Fairmont School and I know about the other schools in the city, I'd say I know some of the teachers. And I know they're good teachers, good people! So I can't see pulling money out of the St. Louis schools and sending it to the county when these children are in the city. You put this money into the schools and improve the schools, not send the children somewhere else to get something, 'cause they can't get any more than what the teachers have to give them; they're not going to get any more out of the school than what they get. If you nurture your kids and push them along, then they're going to get more out of it. If the teachers give them assignments, what not, you come home and you help them to the best of your knowledge. If you can't, then you try to find some way to help them. There are a lot of programs where you can help your kids. There are a lot of study programs and after-school study groups to help them along. So it's really up to the parents how they go about it. Some of them don't know, so the PTA tried to help them know, learn, let them hear about what's going on. That is why I am so involved with the PTA. Fairmont has after-school programs; they have Saturday programs. And this all tends to help the kids along academically.

FAIRMONT ELEMENTARY SCHOOL

When my grandchildren came to stay with us, I wanted them to go to Fairmont because I knew about Fairmont. I knew what a good school it was. Although the city had the deseg [desegregation] plan, I did not want them to go there.

I know a lot of the teachers here in St. Louis. Like I said, Ms. Burroughs at Fairmont was a neighbor of mine. Oh, she's beautiful! I know a lot of her former students, and they are just nuts about her. She's a beautiful person as a teacher. But not only is Ms. Burroughs the best, the teachers and administrators at Fairmont are the best. Mr. Steele treated the teachers right! That is why they stayed so long at the school. He would make sure that the children had everything. That is why my grandchildren and great-grandchildren went there. They would do just about anything for Mr. Steele because he treated the teachers with respect. The people in the school are wonderful for this neighborhood.

When I had my first heart attack, the school took up a collection for me. I really appreciated that!

When Mr. Steele died—I told you that he died a few weeks ago [September 2007], didn't I? There was a caravan of people from everywhere. The whole funeral procession passed through the school, right there on the street that is named after Mr. Steele. Kids came out of the school; it [the funeral procession] was stretched out across the whole street. That was nice.

In 1994, I initially asked Mr. Wooden about Fairmont Elementary School and his expectations for Renee, his granddaughter. Mr. Wooden's goal was for Renee to graduate from high school, attend college, and then have a productive life afterwards. Rather than just allow this to occur without interference, Mr. Wooden was vigilant in providing opportunities for his grandchildren to succeed. He has supported the family on his pension from the military (without any other type of assistance) and made personal and economic sacrifices for the six grandchildren. All of the granddaughters graduated from high school. Five of the six granddaughters graduated from college. The following captures Mr. Wooden's expectations of Renee.

SUCCESS EXPECTED AND FULFILLED

I expect Renee to get a good basis for going to high school and being able to go further in life. Something that will make her think and learn how to use the resources that are offered to her in order to get ahead and to progress. And I am very sure that Fairmont will prepare her to do well at the next level. See, I am very much in love with Fairmont! After she finishes high school and everything, I want her to go on, get her bachelor's and master's. And if she wished to go further, go further, but that's all I have. That's all I think that is necessary.

THE COMMUNITY AND FAIRMONT THROUGH RENEE'S EYES

I first met Renee when she was a student at Fairmont in the fifth grade. I observed her in the classroom, but most of the interaction occurred when I would visit the family's home and see the entire family interacting with one another. Back then, she was a very inquisitive and outgoing child who seemed to enjoy school a lot. The teachers spoke highly of her grandparents' involvement in the school and noted that Renee was very studious. More than a decade later, I interviewed Renee during her senior year in college. She was a senior at a public university in Iowa, studying criminology. As noted earlier, her grandmother, Mrs. Wooden, had relatives who lived in Iowa. One particular relative was instrumental in encouraging Renee to attend school in Iowa.

Renee is about 5 feet 6 inches and a brown-skinned young lady. She was very active in student activities throughout school. Although Renee attended Fairmont Elementary School, she did not attend the neighborhood middle school; instead, she attended a magnet middle school and a magnet high school. Her varied schooling experiences became important in grounding Renee in her own experiences as an African American female, while simultaneously allowing her opportunities for interactions with people across race and social class. The following captures Renee as a young adult in her senior year in college, reflecting on her experiences attending Fairmont and living in the community near the school.

FAIRMONT

What I remember when I was at Fairmont was that I attended the public school directly across the street from my house. The neighborhood was very quiet. Like everybody knew everybody on the block. You know, there weren't many children my age that lived around the part of the community where I lived. The children were from other parts of the community. It was older people like my grandparents on my block. When I think about the teachers, I remember Miss Burroughs, Mr. Miles, and Mr. Hall. Some of the teachers still go back and forth up to Fairmont. I really enjoyed the principal, Mr. Steele. Mr. Steele was great. He was the best principal ever. I mean, he always worked with us through any problems that we may have. I think he was more of a father. He was like a father to everyone that went to Fairmont.

I loved the school! That was one school I actually liked going to. I didn't get tired of school until middle school. But Fairmont School I really liked. I really liked all of the teachers. They all knew me, of course, because I stayed across the street. So I made very good grades at Fairmont.

EDUCATIONAL EXPERIENCES AND CAREER PLANS SINCE FAIRMONT

I did not attend the middle school in the neighborhood because my grandparents did not want me to go there. I went to a magnet middle and high school. I thought the middle and high schools were great schools just because of the diversity within the schools. These schools also had an international focus. I took Chinese, French, and Spanish. These schools also brought me into contact with students from different cultures. When I started thinking about college after I was about to finish high school, the schools that I considered were Jackson State [in Mississippi], Tennessee State, Alabama A&M, Arkansas—Pine Bluff. There were no other schools that I considered. Really! I did not enroll in any of the Black colleges because it's almost like everybody from my high school almost went to Lincoln University. To me, it would just be high school all over again. I got accepted at Lincoln University [in Missouri] and Jackson State University. My sister went to Jackson State, so she hooked me up with some people down there. But I decided to come to Iowa because my grandmother had a family member who worked in admissions. . . . Since I have been here [at my university in Iowa] I have been a member of the Black Student Union. I'm a member of the student support services. I have mentored kids at a high school. My ultimate goal is to work with juvenile delinquents and emotionally disturbed youth. I am considering this area because I see that there are some things that need to be done even in my neighborhood that I grew up in. It has changed a lot. The neighborhood is not as quiet as it used to be when I was growing up there. Some of the older people are not there anymore, and it seems like some of the young children need some guidance, someone to talk to. You know, I have been working with kids all my life. I have a lot of nieces and nephews, and I have had to spend time helping my sisters and grandparents with my nieces and nephews. Just coming home to the neighborhood makes me want to work with youth. Just seeing how the kids are. I just want to talk to them about life.

After graduating from college in December 2005, Renee worked for a year in temporary jobs in St. Louis. She lived with her grandparents while she worked, although she told me that she would have preferred to have had her "own place, but did not want to waste any extra money on an apartment." During the time that she was back at home, Mr. Wooden would drive Renee to her job because she did not have a car. I could tell that while he was proud that she had graduated from college, Mr. Wooden was now hoping that she would go on to graduate school. Renee felt that she was needed at home after graduating to assist her grandfather, who was the primary caretaker for his ailing wife, his mother, and his great-grandchildren. Renee and I talked about her plans since graduating from college. She informed me that she was planning to go to graduate school but needed to take a little time off to develop a plan. I offered my assistance if she felt she needed any advice. But she assured me that she had some ideas about what she wanted to do:

> You know what? I would like to go to graduate school closer to home. I wanted to go down South. But I was trying to think of places where I could go. So, since my sister is in Chicago, I think I would like to be in Chicago. They have a lot of schools to consider there. I don't want to be in St. Louis because I still know that I need to get away. In Chicago, I could stay with my sister, and she just got to the point where she bought her house last October and she is by herself. She doesn't have any kids. That's two of us that don't have any kids [*laughing*]! I am now thinking that I would like to study sociology or social work in grad school. I am going to see what I can do here and then make plans to go to Chicago.

Renee moved to Chicago in 2007. She moved in with her sister Rosalyn and prepared to begin graduate school. Renee is presently a graduate student in sociology at a university in Chicago. On the other hand, Mr. Wooden and I continue to stay in touch, either by telephone or whenever I happen to be in the city. I just call him and he always asks me to stop by.

RESILIENCE AND CHANGE: THE WOODENS VERSUS THE STEREOTYPES

The portrait of Mr. Wooden highlights the complexity of urban African American families' lives, beyond the one-stop views that researchers often paint of such families. There are families in the 'Ville that personify the stereotypical narrative of urban Black families, but there are also families like Mr. Wooden's that defy this narrative. Mr. Wooden's commitment to his family was deeply rooted in his beliefs and experiences about the role of family in the lives of children. For him, the extended family network was essential in the lives of children, as exemplified by his aunt's and great-grandmother's roles in raising him. Mr. Wooden's relatives in Louisiana took care of him until he was able to follow his parents to St. Louis in the late 1940s, which coincided with the Great Black Migration of Black people out of the South to northern and midwestern states in search of greater economic and political opportunities.[1]

Thus when the opportunity arose for Mr. Wooden to become the caretaker for his grandchildren, he did not give it a second thought. Mr.

Wooden's notion of family represents an African American extended family tradition in which other family members—during slavery and afterwards—assumed responsibility for taking care of children whose parents were not able to care for them (Billingsley, 1968, 1992). Such constructions of families should not be viewed solely as a deficit version of a nuclear family; they are merely cultural adaptations to larger social and structural forces that have too often adversely impacted the lives and experiences of African American families. Fortunately for Renee and her siblings, their grandparents served as pillars in their lives, even though they received no additional support from social services such as AFDC (now TANF).

Today, grandparents—particularly those who are low income—are playing an even greater role in caring for their grandchildren, which is further changing traditional notions of school–family relationships. Renee's life chances and educational trajectory benefited from the sacrifices made by her grandparents. They guided her throughout her educational experiences, making sure that she received the best available public schooling opportunities. Moreover, Renee benefited from the social networks available at Fairmont as well as family members who were in the position to further assist in her educational opportunities. This *Black cultural capital* was valuable in Renee's eventual enrollment in college and graduate school.

Like many Black families who desire nice, safe, and well-kept neighborhoods, as well as good schools, Mr. Wooden and his family were part of the first wave of African American families to integrate the neighborhood and school. The community's African American residents adapted the school in such a way that it then began to serve the interests of the African American children who eventually became the predominant population in the school. Although Mr. Wooden initially embraced housing and school integration in the hope of achieving educational and social equality, he later resisted sending his grandchildren into the predominantly White county schools as participants in the St. Louis interdistrict transfer plan. At the middle school level, the magnet component of the desegregation plan, for him, was a better option for Black children in the city.

Finally, the longitudinal nature of the research study in St. Louis provided an opportunity to capture change within the Wooden family—just as I was able to do within the school and community—in order to offer a more complex picture of the experiences of urban Black families. Instead of pathology or deficits, Mr. Wooden's family personifies the resilience of some urban Black families in the midst of the structural forces that impact their lives daily. This kind of depiction of urban Black families as educational advocates for their children rarely occurs in the popular or scholarly portrayals of Black families.

CHAPTER 7

Voices in the Wilderness:
Black Educators on School Reform

Instead of looking principally to the social scientists to demonstrate the adverse consequences of segregation, I would seek to recruit educators to formulate a concrete definition of equality in education, and I would base my argument on that definition.
—Judge Robert Carter, "A Reassessment of *Brown v. Board*"

Black educators are often excluded from the discussion of educational issues facing African American children and their communities. This chapter highlights the value of including these educators' voices in discussions of reforms that specifically focus on the schooling of African American children. Profiled and amplified are the voices of African American educators in St. Louis and Atlanta.

To begin, the chapter provides a historical account of how Black educators' voices were ignored in the debates and discussions surrounding the implementation of *Brown* during the 1960s and 1970s. Years later, a similar omission of Black educators' voices occurred with the implementation of the St. Louis desegregation plan in 1983 and the abandonment of desegregation in Atlanta.

FORGOTTEN VOICES OF BLACK EDUCATORS: A HISTORICAL BACKDROP

Lawyers, social scientists, and members of various civil rights organizations played an integral role in affecting the direction of educational policy for African Americans. They offered their perspectives on what were considered the "damaging effects" of Black children attending legally segregated all-Black schools. Prior to the civil rights campaigns of the 1950s and 1960s, Black educators also assumed a major role in shaping the political and social experiences of African Americans (Franklin, 1990).

Ironically, those Black professionals whose voices were most likely heard in the late 19th and early 20th centuries were ignored as policy makers debated the ways in which *Brown* would be implemented. Throughout the proceedings, analyses, and debates, the potential long-term impact of the implementation of *Brown* on the African American community was often dismissed. Well before *Brown* became law, African Americans vacillated between what was the most effective environment for educating and schooling Black children—separate schools or integrated schools; they showed their understanding of the precarious predicament by favoring one position over the other.

Black educators' support for integration—prior to the *Brown* decision—was conflicted. On one hand, they were compelled to support efforts aimed at eradicating legalized segregation in public schools and the broader society, which could possibly lead to the demise of their careers as Black professionals. In fact, many were ultimately displaced, demoted, and dismissed from the teaching profession once courts and school systems began to enforce *Brown* by desegregating public schools (Etheridge, 1979; Haney, 1978).

On the other hand, these educators did not wholly believe that closing Black schools and enrolling Black children in predominantly White schools would provide them the most effective education (Du Bois, 1935; Johnson, 1954). Many realized that Black children would encounter modified and covert acts of racism in schools that were integrated in student population only, but not in teacher personnel, curricula, and power arrangements. Black educators have always sensed the pulse of the African American community because historically they have been intimately connected with Black families and communities (Anderson, 1988; Foster, 1990, 1997; Morris, 1999; Siddle Walker, 1996).

IN THEIR VOICES TODAY

The educators interviewed in St. Louis were drawn from the three area schools featured in this book: Fairmont Elementary School, Denson Magnet School, and Spring Hill Elementary School. Of the 21 African American educators interviewed in St. Louis, 17 were female and 4 were male; 13 were classroom teachers, 3 were teacher assistants, 2 were principals (male and female), 1 was an interim principal, and 2 were instructional coordinators. Except for the female African American teacher who taught in Spring Hill (Mrs. Mitchell), the educators were all employed in the St. Louis public school system. Although a few had taught between 5 and 10 years, most had been teaching since the St. Louis desegregation plan began in 1983. Four of these educators—all from Fairmont Elementary School—had been teaching or otherwise involved in education for at least 30 years; 1 teacher had taught for the past 42 years.

Almost all of the St. Louis educators were born and raised in St. Louis and attended the segregated public school system. All except two received their teacher training or teaching certification from either Stowe, a historically all-Black teachers college, or Harris–Stowe Teachers College, a merger of Stowe and a historically all-White teachers college, Harris, in 1955, 1 year after *Brown* became law (Wright, 1994). When Harris Teachers College and Stowe Teachers College first merged, the name Stowe was dropped. In 1979, after years of concern expressed by Black alumni of Stowe regarding the omission of their school's name in the merger, the state of Missouri added Stowe to the name of the college.

The Black educators interviewed in Atlanta were all drawn from the ethnographic study of Lincoln Elementary School. Of these educators, seven were females and three were males. Nine of them had attended private Black colleges and universities in Atlanta, institutions that historically have played a major role in educating the city's Black educators (Morris Brown College, Clark Atlanta University, Morehouse College, and Spelman College). Mrs. Jones, the principal at Lincoln, was the only one who attended a public historically Black college or university. These educators' roles in the schools were as follows: seven classroom teachers, one teacher assistant, the principal, and a counselor.

Illustrative of Atlanta's role as an emerging city for Black migrants, the counselor, Dr. Obasi, was from Nigeria. Four of the Black educators in Atlanta had migrated from northern cities, four were born in Atlanta, and one (Ms. Jones, the principal) grew up in southern Georgia. Two of the educators who were born in Atlanta, Ms. Bond and Ms. Murphy, had taught at Lincoln Elementary School for more than 30 years.

Stigmatizing Black Teachers and Schools

The desegregation of public schools after the *Brown* decision drastically affected African American educators. Many were demoted, lost their jobs, or were stigmatized in efforts to desegregate public schools (Foster, 1995; Meier, Stewart, & England, 1989). According to some of the African American educators in St. Louis, remnants of the push to desegregate schools continue to adversely affect the perception of African American teachers and educators today. They have been stigmatized as "unqualified" and "incompetent" in the push to desegregate schools through the transfer plan. Mrs. Burroughs, a teacher at Fairmont Elementary School for 42 years, noted how Black teachers' competency had been challenged since the inception of the transfer plan:

> I have enjoyed teaching Black students. It is bad the way Black teachers have been presented. The busing of Black children out to the county schools has allowed this thinking about Black teachers as incompetent to continue.

Ms. Murphy at Lincoln Elementary School provides a historical example by attesting to the quality of the Black teachers she had when she attended all-Black schools in Atlanta:

> I will never forget how my English teacher, whose husband was M. Carl Holman, who was a historian and later worked with the National Urban Coalition.[1] Mrs. Holman brought out *Julius Caesar* and *Antigone* in our classes. And we shared textbooks in the class. But this teacher taught us in such a way that we read Shakespeare and *Macbeth*; and they came to life! They [the Black educators in the school] just proceeded on. It was a silent, "We shall overcome."

The comments by these educators are insightful. One important message gleaned is their critique of the deeply rooted belief in the larger society that Black schools before *Brown* employed "inferior teachers" who were not preparing Black students properly. This thinking subsequently fueled the notion that Black teachers' "inadequacy" in teaching Black students also disqualified them from teaching White students in racially mixed or predominantly White schools (Foster, 1997). Consequently, although desegregation plans have focused on recruiting students across race, they have not done likewise when it comes to recruiting teachers across race, which was further illustrated by the employment of only one African American teacher (Mrs. Mitchell) at Spring Hill Elementary School.

Closely connected to the stigmatizing of Black educators was the way in which their places of employment were also perceived by the larger White society. The institutions where they worked, even though many of them were grossly underfunded, were also deemed inferior because they enrolled only Black students and employed Black educators. Mr. Steele, the principal at Fairmont Elementary School, asserted that the belief that all-Black schools were inferior, despite some schools' success in educating Black children, persisted and was buttressed by the methods used to publicize the interdistrict transfer plan:

Parents have been sold on the idea, and the school system and the courts have assisted the parents with publicity blitz "school of choice" that the [all-Black] schools in St. Louis are not as good as those in the counties. . . . There would be signs everywhere such as "Do you want your child to go out to a good school?" This used to be advertised in the buses on the placards. They would have "Do you want your child to have a good education? Send him or her to a county school. Call your Voluntary Interdistrict Coordinating Committee." What kind of message is that to send? If you are hit with that, okay, you are going to buy into it. And that is the reason.

As he continued, Mr. Steele drew a parallel between the thrust to persuade Black parents in St. Louis to send their children to the predominantly White county schools and the doll experiment by Kenneth and Mamie Clark, the social scientists whose research was used in the *Brown* case. In this experiment, the Clarks concluded that a handful of Black children's negative preference for the Black dolls (only 14 percent of the students in the sample made anti-Black statements; 86 percent of the students did not) suggested Black "self-hate."

Kenneth Clark was later an expert witness in the *Brown* case. Thus, the conclusion drawn by the Court was that legally segregated Black schools contributed to Black "self-hate" (Cross, 1991). Similar to choosing the White doll over the Black doll, Mr. Steele believed that Black parents and their children were encouraged to choose "White" schools over the "Black" schools—despite the quality and reputation of schools like his. He clearly distinguished between the way the Clarks used their doll example to help eradicate legalized segregation in America and the psychological conditioning that caused some African Americans to value White over Black:

[It is] the same rationale and mentality in why would a Black parent select a predominantly White school. Transform them [the schools] into being dolls. But Kenneth Clark used that argument to say why we need to break it [legal segregation] down. He used it to identify and say this is what's happening. I am only using it the same way to say that this is why parents choose the White schools. It is the same concept when people are going through the same processes, but you are coming to different conclusions. I had a different goal than what he had. He had a goal to integrate schools; mine is to describe why people choose integrated schools.

Finally, Mrs. Collins, a teacher at Denson Magnet School who was twice named "Teacher of the Year" in Missouri, shared her critical perspective. She contended that African American parents bought into the notion that their children would receive a better overall educational experience in the predominantly White county schools. However, she often heard contrary information from Black students who described their experiences and considered returning to the schools in St. Louis.

> My own personal opinion is this: I think African American parents— this is just my perspective—I think they think they [their children] are getting a better education by White teachers; this is not necessarily true. I think that sometimes in going out there, some of the feedback from students that are involved in deseg [the desegregation plan], and they come back just to visit, they tell me, "Mrs. Collins, it is terrible! It's not what we thought it was going to be." Most of them, after a year or two, either they come back into the city or they stay; it depends on the parents. So, I have had numerous kids come back and say, "I'm coming back into the city." They say they just weren't treated fairly. Sometimes the parents think that White is better.

From the perspectives of these African American educators, advertising for the transfer plan explicitly and implicitly perpetuated the belief that Black teachers and the predominantly Black schools in the city were "inferior." According to them, the St. Louis desegregation plan had been promoted by devaluing the quality of education that African American children could receive from schools in the city. Consequently, they asserted that many of the African American parents who sent their children into the predominantly White county schools had been bombarded with misleading "pro-transfer" plan advertisements and were therefore misinformed about what really happened to their children in the county schools. From their perspectives, the massive transferring of African American students into the county schools—partly fueled by misleading information—also had dire consequences for the schools and communities in the city.

The "Creaming" of Black Students

These African American educators—particularly those from Fairmont Elementary School—believed that the desegregation plan in St. Louis disconnected African American students from their communities and the neighborhood schools. They expressed concerns about the extent to which Black children participating in the transfer plan were connected to their neighborhood communities. They also stated that often the high-performing students ended up attending the county schools because of "promises" of a better educational environment. Mrs. Burroughs, a teacher for the past 42 years at Fairmont Elementary School, described how the ability levels of students at her school were not as strong as in previous years: "I would have mostly higher-achieving students and a few lower-achieving students. Now, I might only have a handful of students that are higher-achieving." She attributes part of the change in students' ability levels to the "creaming effect" of students attending the magnet and the county schools. Another teacher who had taught at the neighborhood African American school for 36 years, Mrs. Hall, painfully described the creaming effect of the transfer plan:

> They pulled our best children. . . . They pulled, they took the cream of the crop, basically! So, you know, when a child goes into a magnet school or when he goes into a county school, there are papers that we have to fill out for days and they scrutinize those papers, and if there are things about that child they don't care for, the child shows right back here in public school at Fairmont School.

The perception that African American students were "creamed" away from their neighborhood all-Black schools was held not only by teachers at Fairmont. Mrs. Mitchell, a teacher for 16 years and the only African American teacher at Spring Hill Elementary School, shared this view:

> The drawback to the transfer plan is that it takes the African American children out of their neighborhoods. They really don't have a good connection; they really feel isolated being out here. That's what I think, and I really believe in going to your school in your neighborhood; you get to know the people better and you get to know friends.

Whereas Mrs. Mitchell and the other educators have noted the drawbacks of the plan, the following section examines the extent to which these educators feel that the plan has benefited Black students.

Benefits for White and Black Students

When White children attend racially desegregated public schools, it is often their first exposure to children from different racial and ethnic backgrounds. This fact has been presented as one of the primary benefits of public school desegregation (in Supreme Court *amicus curiae* briefs), and it was echoed by Mrs. Ross, an African American grandparent:

> The problem is that they [White people] are not used to being around Black people. This is the way it is for the [White] teachers and the children. . . . The White children have benefited from being around the have-nots; my children are the have-nots. A lot of the White children are the haves. They benefit in knowing that my child is just as bright as they are.

The interdistrict transfer plan exposed White students to a group of students who were racially and economically different from them, thereby allowing them to see that some children, in the words of one educator, "did not live like them."

Overall, research based on standardized test scores has not conclusively shown that African American students benefited academically from attending desegregated schools with their middle-class White counterparts. However, advocates are suggesting the need to look beyond short-term effects or measures of desegregation such as test scores by focusing on the long-term consequences, such as Black students' occupational aspirations and access to opportunities, of attending desegregated schools.

Debates abound regarding the extent to which Black children benefited from the St. Louis interdistrict transfer plan. For example, a report from the Voluntary Interdistrict Coordinating Council (VICC)—the office responsible for coordinating the St. Louis transfer plan—revealed that test scores for African American students who transferred into the county schools were relatively the same as those for African American students who remained in the all-Black schools in the city of St. Louis. Furthermore, a report by the Citizens' Commission on Civil Rights (1997), an organization based in Washington, D.C., concluded that African American students who attended schools in the county had higher graduation rates than African American students who attended schools in the city.

However, this report did not control for socioeconomic status—a known mitigating factor affecting the school experiences of students. For instance, whereas 94 percent of the Black students in the regular city schools received free or reduced lunches, 76 percent of the Black students who transferred into the county schools received them.

Although not noted in the report by the Citizens' Commission, African American students who attended magnet schools had higher graduation rates than those who attended either city schools or county schools. When asked about the extent to which she felt that the desegregation plan

. . .

had benefited Black children, Mrs. Woodson, principal of Denson Magnet School, responded: "Yes, they [magnet schools] are beneficial to all children. This could have been done in all-Black schools; I think any progressive educator would believe that."

Mrs. Woodson noted that her school had benefited from the transfer plan's financial support of the magnet school, as well as from the quality of her teachers. Her point, however, was that the support given to magnet schools should originally have been designed for the all-Black schools in the city—without having to try to "entice" White suburban families to send their children to the magnet schools. Mrs. Bethune, the instructional coordinator at Denson Magnet School, said, "It [the transfer plan] also was so that White children could be educated with Black children. That was the intent, which was good. But somewhere along the line that was forgotten."

White parents in the county schools, who rarely exercised the option of sending their children to the magnet schools in the city, ignored the noble intent expressed by Mrs. Woodson. Only 1,478 White students transferred into magnet schools in St. Louis during the 1997–1998 academic year. And since the program has been in place, and later modified, the White student enrollment in the magnet schools has been approximately 1,500 students annually from the participating school districts. As noted later, the numbers have decreased substantially since the new settlement that was agreed upon in 1999.

This difficulty in desegregating with magnet schools was also experienced by Kansas City schools, where desegregation funds focused on turning many inner-city and predominantly Black schools into magnet schools as a way to attract White students back into the city's public school system. The plan was ultimately abandoned because so few White parents chose to send their children to the schools and because there was no significant change in students' test scores (see *Missouri v. Jenkins*, 1995).

The extent to which Black children benefited academically from transferring into the county schools was not clear, even among the African American educators. The magnet schools were well funded and received additional resources because they were used to desegregate students. In addition, these extra funds also allowed for some of the all-Black students in the St. Louis schools to be assured of adequate educational resources.

However, the major financial beneficiaries of the desegregation plan have been the county schools. The impact of the transfer plan on the overall revenue for the county districts cannot be ignored. For example, the Homewood School District, where Mrs. Mitchell taught, received approximately $68 million by participating in the transfer plan from 1984 through 1993. The county districts received a per-pupil expenditure for each Black student transferring into their respective districts, in addition to half the amount of state aid for each of the approximately 1,478 county students who had transferred to city magnet schools. Consequently, buildings have been constructed and staff and faculty were hired using these funds. Although there have been some financial benefits for Black students who attended the magnet schools, the predominantly White county districts benefited financially by participating in the plan.

CONSEQUENCES OF ENDING DESEGREGATION

Some desegregation experts and policy analysts highly encouraged the continuation of the desegregation plans because they believed that the plans offered African American students from the inner city greater educational opportunities than the schools in the city and slowly chipped away at the color line between Whites in the suburbs and African Americans in the city (Wells & Crain, 1997). In particular, Gary Orfield has been concerned that the "dismantling of desegregation" would result in the resegregation of the city schools and, once again, high concentrations of minority and low-income schools (Orfield & Eaton, & the Harvard Project, 1996).

Some scholars (Boger & Orfield, 2005; Orfield & Lee, 2007) have specifically noted how the phenomenon of public school resegregation is especially occurring in the U.S. South. These researchers attribute this to housing and demographic patterns, such as African Americans' return migration to the South, as well as to the end of school desegregation through the declaration of unitary status—a legal term meaning that school districts have asserted that they have done all they could to create racial balance and will not revert to prior segregation practices. These scholars believe that the Supreme Court's recent ruling in *Parents Involved in Community Schools v. Seattle School District No. 1* (2007), which struck down the use of race to promote school desegregation, will only exacerbate this resegregation.

Mrs. Jones, the principal at Lincoln Elementary School in Atlanta, witnessed the beginning of this resegregation in a racially integrated school where she had previously been the guidance counselor. Prior to coming to Lincoln as the principal, Mrs. Jones had worked as a guidance counselor in a southern Georgia town (in Chatham County) that had a desegregation plan in place. The particular school had a 60/40 White-to-Black student population. Mrs. Jones said that the school system attained unitary status after the NAACP and the school district agreed to release the district from a desegregation Court order, as long as Chatham County said that it would continue with desegregation efforts. Although leaders in the

school system agreed to make a "good faith effort" to keep desegregation in place, Mrs. Jones did not believe that this good faith effort would
continue:

> I don't believe that people will do what they say that they will do.
> Since 1998, I have seen the schools gradually take a turn in which
> the schools in the inner city have gone from being primarily
> African American and the schools on the outskirts of town are now
> primarily Caucasian American. And the Black children who are
> there [on the outskirts of town] are usually the children of those
> who are able to live in those surrounding areas.

On the other hand, some of the African Americans in St. Louis questioned the merits of continuing to desegregate in that city by transferring
African American students into the predominantly White and county
schools (Mannies, 1993). They have been especially critical of the fact that
almost $2 billion had gone into financing the plan, with a significant
amount going toward transportation and a per-pupil expenditure to the
county schools for each African American transfer student.

These Black educators' views, however, varied about whether to end
or continue desegregation. Some believed that, given the necessary financial resources and support, Black children could still receive a quality education in primarily African American school environments. Others believed
that there was some merit in maintaining racial balances in the schools.
Seemingly ironic, Mrs. Mitchell, the only African American teacher at the
county school, embraced the former view:

> If the desegregation plan [in St. Louis] ended today, I think that I
> would be sad. But to another extent, I would only relish it if the
> inner-city schools, the schools were redone, new books were
> bought, and the conditions were like they should be in any school
> when they sent them [the African American students] back.

Some of these African American educators expressed concerns regarding how the material conditions and funding of the city schools, as well as
the racial balancing of students, would be affected by ending the plan.
While they acknowledged the importance for Black children of being exposed to children from various racial and ethnic backgrounds, some did
not believe that racial balancing was essential for the quality education of
Black children. They maintained that Black children could receive a quality education in a predominantly Black school that was adequately funded

and supported. These educators' perspectives resonated deeply with elements of critical race theory (CRT), and they were the most skeptical of the plan. Elements of CRT were embedded throughout the interviews with these Black educators. The *interest-conversion dilemma* of CRT—which is grounded in the notion that significant progress for African Americans is achieved only when the goals of Blacks are consistent with the needs of Whites—was apparent in the manner in which the educators talked about desegregation.

A significant number of African American students transferred into the predominantly White county schools, in comparison with White students who participated in the city's magnet school program. The disparity between Black students' and White students' participation rates, and the desegregation settlement's low expected goal for suburban students to attend magnet schools, may be partly explained by Bell's (1980) argument that "Whites will not support civil rights policies that appear to threaten their superior social status" (214–215). He termed this *the price of racial remedies*. Although the integration of Black students into the predominantly White county might have represented to African Americans a step toward greater social and educational justice, many White families hesitated to disrupt their status by sending their children to the city's magnet schools just so racial balancing could occur. For these parents, racial balance and equality were secondary to ensuring a quality education for their children.

In an unspoken way, many of the White parents in the St. Louis counties were reluctant to lose this White privilege by associating with those institutions and people who do not represent and reify their Whiteness solely for the advancement of civil rights. For example, the magnet schools had to entice White parents to send their children into the city schools with the reassurance that these schools were unlike the predominantly Black schools that existed in the city. Their children's attendance at predominantly Black schools, despite a particular school's quality, would have represented a loss of "White" status (Harris, 1993). The transfer plan was conceptualized and implemented in such a way that this racial reality was recognized; the only way to make some White parents consider sending their children to the city schools would be to make these schools "exceptional without question."

White students' presence in the city schools automatically ascribed a greater sense of value to the St. Louis public school system. Unfortunately, this valuing of "Whiteness" resulted in a simultaneous devaluing of Black people and their institutions, particularly by the manner in which advertising promoted the county schools at the expense of the all-Black city schools and African American educators.

CONCLUSION: HEARING BLACK EDUCATORS' VOICES

Overall, these African American educators remind the scholarly and policy communities of the African American community's multiple views on *Brown v. Board of Education* and how the racial balancing of schools was to accomplish one set of objectives. For them, the implementation of *Brown* also should have been about African Americans having greater political and economic control of the education of Black students. As this chapter illustrates, the conceptualization and implementation of educational policies—particularly those with serious implications for African American education—are incomplete when they ignore the perspectives of Black educators. The voices of these educators provide a more inclusive, but often neglected, perspective on educational policy for African American children. When researchers and policy makers begin to fully chronicle and thoroughly understand the overall implications and ramifications of desegregation policy for Black people—which includes hearing the voices of Black educators— then the real promises of *Brown* may become more fully realized.

CHAPTER 8

Fulfilling the Promise of Quality Schooling for Black Children

As evidenced from the empirical findings presented throughout this book, the schooling of low-income African American children in the urban centers of the United States has been filled with paradoxes, perils, and promise. Too often, the promises were broken, particularly *Brown*'s promise of quality schooling (Irons, 2002). Du Bois's (1935) analysis of the "separate Black school/mixed school" paradox still rings true at the dawn of the 21st century. Millions of African American children continue to attend predominantly Black schools. Consequently, improving the education of these children must focus not only on the schools that, in theory, would appear to be "ideal" for all children to attend. Instead, educators, researchers, and policy makers must research, understand, and improve those schools that low-income Black children presently attend.

The scholarly, policy, and educational communities are all too familiar with the perils that low-income Black children face in underresourced schools and neglected communities. Well documented are the high teacher turnover rates, the continued lack of resources—despite living in the wealthiest country in the world—and the myriad other social issues that disproportionately and adversely affect low-income African American children. But these schools, and the communities where they are located, would not be this way if there were the national, state, and local will to make them better, thereby enhancing low-income Black children's chances for educational and social success.

The need to improve urban and predominantly Black schools is imperative. But it is also important to remember that the predominantly Black schools in U.S. urban centers are not the only places where low-income Black children experience educational perils. As the chapters on Denson Magnet School and Spring Hill Elementary School illustrated, these children faced other kinds of perils in racially diverse and predominantly White suburban schools. These perils had to do not so much with a lack of resources as with the lack of access to these resources for African American students, as well as the disregard for African American people, their culture, and the experiences they brought into the schools.

Although Black children are presented with promises before attending these schools their perils in racially diverse and predominantly White schools include disproportionate disciplinary actions, academic tracking into low-level classes, and overrepresentation in special education. These outcomes emanate from (1) educators' low expectations of Black children's academic and intellectual abilities, (2) the deculturalizing of African American children in classrooms, and (3) the power imbalance that Black students and families experience in these schools.

Too often, low-income Black children find themselves in an educationally perilous situation across different types of schools. The educational salvation of low-income Black children necessitates a multisided approach to minimizing the perils these children experience. Similar to a math problem, one has to simultaneously solve both sides of the equation to arrive at a solution (Hale, 2001). Predominantly White, racially diverse, and predominantly Black schools all have to better serve Black children.

By illuminating predominantly Black schools that successfully educated urban and low-income African American children, this book deviated from most popular portrayals and scholarly investigations of urban schools and African American education. Given the entrenched racial patterns in the United States in terms of housing and wealth as well as the racial stigmatization that African Americans continue to experience, low-income Black children will continue to attend urban schools that are predominantly Black. Lincoln Elementary School and Fairmont Elementary School revealed the promise that some of these schools hold when there is a serious commitment from policy makers, school administrators, educators, community members, and parents to improving the education of low-income Black children.

TOWARD A CONCEPTUAL UNDERSTANDING OF COMMUNALLY BONDED SCHOOLS

What do the insights presented in this book mean for the way the scholarly and policy communities think about schooling Black children in general and low-income urban Black children in particular? The findings in this book suggest a need for the scholarly and policy communities to move beyond existing theoretical views of involving low-income Black families in their children's schooling and to begin to think deeply about how the interplay of social class and race influences the extent to which these families and children are able to gain access to social and cultural capital in particular school settings. This book—specifically the chapter on Spring Hill Elementary School—highlighted how race and poverty adversely influenced the extent to which low-income African American families were able to make connections with other more resource-rich groups—and thereby accrue social capital.

Educators, scholars, and policy makers need to reframe the conventional view about the extent to which increased social capital in urban and predominantly African American communities and schools will lead to enhanced educational experiences and an overall improved quality of life for low-income African American families. Specifically, social capital theorists believe that individuals accrue benefits as a result of their ties to others (Bourdieu, 1986; Coleman, 1987, 1988; Dika & Singh, 2002). Embracing Coleman's view of social capital as positive social control based on trust and information channels, a number of scholars have suggested that low-income and minority families can acquire social capital when families, communities, and schools work together in the interest of students (see Cibulka & Kritek, 1996). Although scholars have recently applied the concept of social capital to the urban school reform debate, this concept was also a major assumption of public school desegregation policies during the 1970s, 1980s, and 1990s.

For instance, throughout the United States, desegregation plans were premised on the notion that African American students would receive greater access to resources and information networks in middle-class, predominantly White schools. Consequently, Black children would then have opportunity paths and outcomes similar to those of White, middle-class students. However, these discussions of social capital were often devoid of a critical analysis of the conditions that are conducive to creating greater access to social capital for low-income African American families and students, thereby minimizing the educational perils facing Black students.

Two presuppositions about the acquisition of social capital emerged from the studies presented in this book. First, in a society stratified by race and class, such as the United States, there are indelible negative perceptions of the capabilities and the moral fiber of the subordinated social group (usually low-income African Americans). For example, there is the assumption that African American culture and institutions are inadequate in cultivating Black educational success. Second, social groups in power (across race or ethnicity) can choose whether to associate with the subordinated group or whether to allow the subordinated group to benefit from the social capital in the particular setting where the dominant group's power resides. These suppositions are applicable not only to schooling but also to the broader society, as exemplified by recent housing policy targeting low-income Black families.

Moreover, recent discussions surrounding social capital theory have been premised on the notion that African American institutions were never connected to families and communities. As numerous scholars have noted, historically, all-Black schools were integrally connected with African American families and communities (Anderson, 1978; Dempsey & Noblit, 1993; Morris & Morris, 2002; Siddle Walker, 1996). In many ways, desegregation policies fractured this relationship. These policies were grounded in the notion that Black students would receive equal education and have greater access to resources and information networks (social capital) if they attended middle-class, predominantly White schools. Unfortunately, many Black students who attended such schools did not benefit from the social capital within these schools. They became faced with new educational perils: tracked into low-level classes (Lucas, 1999; Lucas & Berends, 2007; Oakes, 1985), marginalized, and disproportionately disciplined (Meier, Stewart, & England, 1989; Monroe, 2005).

In addition, White people have historically resisted educating their children in schools that enrolled significant Black student populations. This was made apparent by the swift departure of White people from the communities and public schools of St. Louis and Atlanta during the late 1960s and 1970s when public school desegregation eventually became enforced, the increasingly low participation of White students in the St. Louis desegregation plan (in the fall of 2008, only 178 White students from the original 16 participating White counties attended city magnet schools), and the reluctance by White people who recently moved into the Lincoln community in Atlanta to consider Lincoln Elementary School as an educational option for their children. Their presence in the school would have contributed to the school becoming a "naturally integrated" school.

Consequently, social capital theory, as articulated by Coleman (1987, 1988), is limited in terms of its applicability to African Americans' social and educational experiences because it ignores (1) the significance of White people's self-interest, (2) how race and racism affect the extent to which Black people can acquire social capital in predominantly White school settings (on the role of context, see Lareau & Horvat, 1999), and (3) the sociohistorical experiences of Black people, particularly the connections that Black schools have historically had with local Black communities and families.

A mainstay of Black people's historical experiences in U.S. society has been in the deep connection to the institutions in which they participated, whether by force or because of their unique cultural experiences. Historically, Black institutions, such as churches, schools, families, communities, and social societies, were interdependent, reflective of historical and cultural patterns as well as the social and legal restrictions that limited Black participation in the broader U.S. society (Billingsley, 1992). The relations between Black people and institutions transcended rigidly defined roles and were communal in nature. Out of these social and historical experiences, a certain consciousness fostered what anthropologists term a "fictive kinship"—a sense of peoplehood or collective identity—due to Black people's continued subordination in U.S. society (see Fordham, 1996). As a result of this kinship (i.e., Black racial identity), Black people shared their cultural capital with one another and developed their social capital (Black social capital) for survival and success in a "world" bounded by the omnipresent forces of racism and discrimination—forces that limited their opportunities beyond the segregated world (Orr, 1999).

Bourdieu's (1986) articulation of social capital as a status-reproducing agent explains how "Whiteness," as an ideology, ensured its overarching domination of Black society and schooling, historically and contemporarily. And yet, amid adverse structural forces, Black people displayed agency; they collectively used their social and cultural capital to positively shape Black students' schooling experiences. Therefore, it is not totally accurate for some sociologists of education to describe urban and low-income African Americans' schooling and community experiences primarily within a structuralist framework—a framework that too often relegates African American people to the role of nonactors. Instead, as the ethnographic investigations in this book reveal, a sense of agency among African Americans became expressed within these deterministic conditions.

When applied to African American schooling, social capital theory can be greatly informed by a sociohistorical understanding of African Americans' experiences, which takes into account the role of race and the permanence of racism in U.S. society (see Bell, 1987, 1992). Furthermore, it becomes imperative that discussions of social capital theory and African American schooling also consider the agency and sustenance that are characteristic of African American people, culture, and institutions—apart from and in response to oppressive forces. The notion of *communally bonded schools* builds on the above analyses of social capital theory by incorporating the strengths and traditions of African American institutions as a key step toward creating effective educational reform for low-income African American students.

COMMUNALLY BONDED SCHOOLS AS A FRAMEWORK FOR BLACK EDUCATIONAL PRACTICE

In 1973, African American and White officials in the Atlanta public school system and the city of Atlanta agreed to what became known as the "Second Atlanta Compromise." At the end of the 2006–2007 academic year, the Atlanta public school system enrolled approximately 49,773 students, down from an enrollment figure of 55,812 students in 2001–2002. Of these students, 85 percent were African American and 75 percent were low-income. White students made up about 9 percent of the total student population, which was an increase from previous years, partly due to the drop in the total African American student population.

In search of better housing and schooling opportunities, many middle-income and some low-income African American families left Atlanta for nearby suburbs such as Clayton County and DeKalb County. African Americans' movement over the past three decades, in large measure, has been out of urban centers and into suburban communities. For instance, in 1970, 60 percent of African Americans lived in central cities and 19 percent lived in suburban communities. In 2002, however, 51 percent of African Americans lived in metropolitan areas inside central cities and 36 percent lived in the suburbs (U.S. Census Bureau, 2002; see also U.S. Census Bureau, 2005).

Some of the increased African American presence in suburban areas near Atlanta has been a function of federal housing policies such as HOPE VI[1] and Section 8, which have provided some low-income families with housing vouchers to move into what are commonly called the inner-rings of suburbs. In these new places of residence, however, low-income African American families and their children are encountering a new set of community and schooling dynamics, which have yet to be fully explored by researchers. Still, others remain in cities. The changing nature of metropolitan areas, particularly African Americans' outward migration into suburbia, is challenging the conventional urban/suburban binary. In metropolitan areas such as Atlanta, the suburbs are increasingly characterized by a predominantly Black public school population and economic diversity.

Until there are some systemic changes in the United States, a pragmatic scholarly and policy approach would entail better understanding those urban and predominantly African American schools that show promise. At Fairmont and Lincoln, in particular, some of the positive characteristics in these schools were consistent with findings from historical case studies of all-Black segregated schools (Dempsey & Noblit, 1993; Jones, 1981; Morris & Morris, 2002; Savage, 1998; Siddle Walker, 1996, 2000) as well as studies on the role of Black educators in these schools (Beauboeuf-La Fontant, 1999; Foster, 1997; Franklin, 1990; King, 1993). The following key characteristics embody the notion of communally bonded schools.

School Personnel Reaching Out to Families

School personnel at Fairmont Elementary School and Lincoln Elementary School actively reached out to the low-income to working-class African

American families, creating a climate of trust that encouraged and fostered opportunities for families to actively participate in school events. Today, schools and educators have to mitigate those barriers that prevent low-income parents from feeling they are not a part of their children's schools (Comer, 1980; Edwards, 1996; Epstein, 1992; Morris, 1999). Teachers should invite African American parents back to school in a manner that reflects mutual respect and understanding of the social and cultural experiences of African American families and communities (Edwards, 1996). School personnel have to create trusting relationships with African American families similar to those that were typically found in segregated Black schools (Dempsey & Noblit, 1993; Edwards, 1996; Siddle Walker, 1996).

Intergenerational and Cultural Bonding

The relations between school personnel and families at Lincoln and Fairmont were intergenerational and culturally reaffirming. Senior teachers played essential roles in setting the expectations regarding students' academic performance, sustaining traditions, developing an appreciation of African American culture, and cultivating a sense of community among the staff and faculty. Furthermore, the bonds between the families and educators reflected not only a fulfillment of their ascribed roles but also a genuine commitment to educating the African American students. The bonds between the teachers (most of whom were African American) and the students were parent-like in nature, as previously described by Michele Foster (1997) and Jacqueline Jordan Irvine (1990) in their studies of African American teachers' relationships with students. Across generations, families maintained a persistent confidence in the ability of each school to educationally prepare their children.

Significant Presence of Black Teachers in the School

The integral role that African American educators historically played in the schooling of Black children, and the role played by educators in the four schools discussed in this book, should not be minimized or ignored. This does not mean that *all* African American teachers effectively teach African American children or that some White teachers cannot effectively teach Black children. Those White teachers at Fairmont and Lincoln, and those described by scholars such as Ladson-Billings (1994), valued and affirmed African American children's culture and prepared them educationally, but such teachers are rare. White teachers, who make up 90 percent of the teaching force in the United States, will continue to teach African American and other racial and ethnic minority children. Unfortunately, fewer than half of these teachers participate in professional development related to managing a diverse classroom and working with diverse students (National Education Association, 2003). Furthermore, more than 40 percent of the public schools in the United States have no minority teachers on staff, although they often have a significant number of minority students.

African American teachers, on the other hand, represent approximately 6 percent of the total public school teaching force in the United States (National Center for Education Statistics, 2003; National Education Association, 2003), which is the lowest percentage since 1971—which coincides with the implementation of many public school desegregation plans. Yet African American teachers are *more likely* than White teachers to teach in economically impoverished and predominantly African American schools (Gay, 1997), least likely to expel and suspend Black children, least likely to place Black children in lower-track and special education courses (Serwatka, Deering, & Grant, 1995), and more likely to have positive academic achievement gains with Black children (Dee, 2001; Irvine, 1990; Rubovitz & Maehr, 1973). By highlighting the Black educators across the four schools, this book contributes to the corpus of scholarship that provides longitudinal evidence on the effectiveness of Black teachers in teaching Black children (see Anderson, 1988; Beauboeuf-La Fontant, 1999; Du Bois, 1935; Foster, 1997; Franklin, 1990; Irvine & Irvine, 1983; King, 1993; Ladson-Billings, 1994; Siddle Walker, 2000).

Chapter 5, as well as previous research (Morris, 2004), captured how the educators (many of whom were African American and originally from lower socioeconomic backgrounds) had a deep and trusting relationship with African American students and their families as well as how the parents felt that the educators really cared about them and understood their situation. Like other effective teachers of low-income African American children, the educators at Fairmont and Lincoln saw themselves as having life experiences similar to those of the children they taught and strongly identified with the communities where they taught. Some grew up in predominantly African American and low-income communities or had relatives who once lived in these communities.

Ferguson (1998a, 1998b) reviewed the evidence on the effects of matching Black teachers with Black students and concluded that the evidence is mixed. For example, he noted that research by Alexander, Entwisle, and Thompson (1987)—which analyzed data from 20 Baltimore schools in the 1982–1983 schoolyear—revealed that "the best results for Black students, especially in mathematics, were associated with Black teachers of low socioeconomic status and White teachers of high socioeconomic status" (Ferguson, 1998b, p. 349). Ferguson asserted that it is plausible that low-status Black teachers and high-status White teachers (in comparison to high-status Black teachers and low-status White teachers) are most comfortable with Black children and are more inclined to believe that these children can learn. Thus, it is possible that an African American teacher can make a difference for Black children, but more so if that African American teacher understands and identifies with the social-class experiences of the children that he or she teaches.

Black Principals as Bridges and Cultural and Academic Leaders

The African American principals at the two predominantly Black schools in this book bridged the school with the community and outside agencies, reminiscent of the roles that Black principals historically assumed in segregated schools. Dr. Frazier and Mr. Steele created high expectations for students and teachers, solidified the school with the community, and ensured that students and teachers had the resources to succeed. They were not only academic leaders but also cultural leaders who understood how race and culture shaped African American schooling (Dillard, 1995).

While policy makers are pressing for greater accountability through the elimination of principal tenure, they should not ignore the history of Black schooling in which African American principals played a major role in sustaining Black schools over time. Given that two of the three African American principals profiled, as well as the instructional coordinators at three of these schools (Denson, Fairmont, and Lincoln), were African American females, future research efforts especially need to highlight the intersection of race and gender in contemporary African American school leaders' experiences (Benham, 1997; Dillard, 1995, 2000; Loder, 2002).

The African American school leaders in three of the schools (Mrs. Jones, Mr. Steele, Mrs. Woodson, and Mrs. Bethune) were ardent advocates for Black children's education. This was particularly significant in the case of Denson Magnet School, where Mrs. Woodson and Mrs. Bethune fervently fought for Black children to be placed into the school's gifted education program because they understood that it was not enough for African American children to just attend a racially diverse magnet school; these students needed to benefit from what these schools had to offer. Whether they attend predominantly Black, predominantly White, or racially diverse schools, African American children need administrators who can advocate on their behalf in order to ensure their success within these different types of schools. They especially need administrators and educators who identify with African American families and children and understand their unique circumstances and experiences. This identification with Black people and their institutions is a critical component of communally bonded schools.

African American Schools as Pillars in Black Communities

Like other schools that have successfully educated low-income African American children from inner-city communities (e.g., Hilliard, 2003; Scheurich, 1998), Fairmont and Lincoln had excellent principals, committed teachers, a love ethic for Black children, and were strongly connected to the communities where these children lived. Fairmont and Lincoln functioned as stabilizing forces for the communities—a role similar to the one that Black churches and schools historically played in supporting African American families and communities (Anderson, 1988; Irvine & Irvine, 1983; Lincoln & Mamiya, 1990). The relationship of each school to its respective community developed out of the schools' and communities' shared history. If supported financially and politically, such schools may demonstrate promise in the promotion of healthy urban communities.

But will educational leaders and national, state, and local politicians give their full support to improving urban and predominantly Black schools, without worrying about the political consequences? A true commitment to improving the education of these children will require every level of government to take on the crisis facing African American students throughout schools in the United States with the same kind of intensity with which political and economic leaders approached the economic crisis in the United States in the fall of 2008. There cannot be a "survival of the fittest" approach when it comes to educating urban and low-income children in public schools, particularly when the participants who are Black have been historically disenfranchised and then provided with few opportunities to truly catch up. They, too, need a bailout package that ensures that they will thrive in, rather than just survive, U.S. public schooling.

Moreover, housing reform is inextricably linked to educational reform. As urban areas have undergone transformations as a result of gentrification and policies such as HOPE VI, community stakeholders would do well to factor in the stabilizing role of schools for local communities. To make cities and communities better, schools have to also become better. According to Judge Robert L. Carter (1996), who as a lawyer was primarily responsible for conceptualizing the litigation and drafting the court documents for *Brown*, "Whatever is accomplished in isolated areas of the country, the metropolitan centers are where a majority of blacks now resides, and the schools in these centers must provide equal education for minority children" (p. 23).

Providing an equal education for African American students also has to include ensuring that African American families and children are active and valued participants in the overall culture and community in schools. Mrs. Hall, a teacher at Fairmont Elementary School, described the school's connection with families and community members, drawing a parallel between the stabilizing role of Fairmont today and the role that Black churches historically played in Black communities: "A community is only as good as the school that is in it. The basis of the Black community used to be the Black church. Fairmont has served an essential role, just as the Black church has played in the African American community."

SUPPORTING THE MIXED-SCHOOL MODEL

African American children continue to attend schools that are racially diverse or predominantly White, despite the Supreme Court's 2007 ruling against the use of race to promote public school desegregation. For instance, key stakeholders in St. Louis and the state of Missouri developed a plan that allowed Black students from St. Louis public school system to continue their enrollment in the suburban districts if they so desired, thus providing African American parents with an educational option beyond the schools in the city. Other metropolitan areas such as Louisville, Kentucky, have also modified their plans to ensure that children will continue to have opportunities to attend racially diverse schools.

The Missouri legislature developed a plan to offset the city's loss of court-ordered state funding and to continue its desegregation efforts in St. Louis with a long-term funding remedy: Senate Bill 781, which became law in August 1998. This law revised the state funding formula and required St. Louis voters to pay an additional local tax to support the St. Louis public schools. A three-member "overlay" board was an outgrowth of this law, and it determined that the tax increase should occur in the form of sales taxes, rather than property taxes, so as to have individuals who use the services of the city also pay taxes.

On February 2, 1999, the voters in St. Louis approved a two-thirds-of-a-cent sales tax increase. This tax increase raised the sales tax from 6.85 percent to 7.51 percent on goods and services sold in St. Louis after July 1, 1999. The sales tax was expected to increase local school revenue for St. Louis by approximately $23 million. This amount would be matched by state funds in the amount of $40 million, which still would leave the district approximately $7 million short of the amount that it would normally have received from the 1983 settlement.

On March 12, 1999, the judges on the case signed the order officially ending the 1983 settlement in St. Louis. In removing the case from federal supervision, they agreed to the following: (1) to continue the transfer plan during the next 3 years for African American students who wished to transfer into the county schools. At the end of the third year, citizens from each participating suburban school district would vote on whether to continue or to end the plan in their respective school districts. (2) To provide additional state funds to the St. Louis Public School District for the purpose of expanding magnet school opportunities to White and Black students in the city via a change in the state funding formula and the tax increase. (3) To provide money for capital improvement in the city schools over the next 10 years. To facilitate the new transfer plan, a nonprofit agency, the Voluntary Interdistrict Choice Corporation (VICC), replaced the Voluntary Interdistrict Coordinating Council.

The new settlement allowed for new students to be admitted to the voluntary transfer plan and the St. Louis magnet schools through the 2008–2009 academic year. Over this period of time, enrollment goals were set that would allow specified percentages of students to continue participating in the plan. During the first 3 years after the new settlement, the districts collectively agreed to maintain at least 85 percent of 1998–1999 enrollment, with a future target of at least 70 percent.

From 2005 forward, no minimum enrollment had to occur. Beginning in September 2008, 6,774 St. Louis African American students were attending county schools, but only 171 students from the participating county schools attended the magnet school programs in St. Louis. In addition, the rules that govern No Child Left Behind (NCLB) in terms of subgroups' academic performance may also be affecting districts' decisions to accept fewer Black students each year. Because the Black students have traditionally not performed at high levels, some districts may be choosing to limit the numbers of transfer Black students in order to achieve adequate yearly progress (AYP) from year to year.

Moreover, a couple of the districts originally participating in the St. Louis interdistrict transfer plan no longer participated because of greater minority student presence in the district due to demographic shifts. To reduce busing costs, four attendance zones were created in the city with links to specific suburban school districts. VICC received $50 million to cover the transportation costs associated with facilitating the transfer of students within the new attendance zones.

Since the ethnographic research in the suburban school, Spring Hill, some county schools now offer promising programs to ease African Americans' transition into the schools. Such programs have included workshops that focused on understanding African American students, the achievement gap, enriching race relations, and gender-specific programs that targeted African American males and females. These and similar programs are important for African American students' educational success, considering that in June 2007, the VICC board approved a 5-year extension that allowed transfer students to be enrolled in the county districts until the 2013–2014 schoolyear. The mixed-school model (initially as racially diverse magnet schools and increasingly as racially diverse suburban schools as a result of Black families' outward migration to suburbs) will continue to play a role in shaping African American children's education and identity.

However, African Americans' increasing presence in suburban areas does not automatically confer middle-class status on them. Sometimes these families rent apartments in the suburban communities, hoping to give their children what they perceive to be a better education. What this suggests is that the notion of "urban" as a geographical context will have to increasingly consider the presence of once-urbanized residents in new suburban contexts. The enrollment of low-income Black children in suburban and more middle-income schools does not necessarily mean equitable treatment when they are there; ensuring that these children truly benefit from all that these schools have to offer is of major concern. School administrators and teachers play a critical role in ensuring equitable schooling opportunities for these children.

In terms of African American parents' roles, their reasons for choosing a particular school for their children have to go beyond looking only at the racial composition of the school or its physical structure; the choice should be based more on the educators' success in working with Black children. As Du Bois noted in 1935, "there is no magic." Too often, African American parents have chosen to send their children to suburban schools because of the purported resources at these schools and merely because these schools were suburban and predominantly White.

The African American parents profiled in this book who sent their children to Spring Hill Elementary School had never visited the school prior to their children's enrollment. They chose the "White" school hoping that it would provide a better intellectual experience for their children. Yet the sociocultural and psychological dimensions of educating Black children were ignored. These parents did not fully consider the psychological aspects of their children's education. They, like many others, considered only the material aspects of the schooling process.

While the ethnographic investigation of Spring Hill Elementary School highlights the early years of schooling low-income Black students in predominantly White and middle class schools, the vulnerability of Black children at this point is greatest, and therefore the psychological toll of low expectations could become cumulative. Therefore, when statistics in predominantly White suburban schools show that Black high school students are not achieving well in relation to White students (see Ogbu, 2003), one must understand what most likely happened to Black children at their earlier and most formative years in these schools, thus setting the path for lower expectations throughout the educational pipeline.

For example, researchers affiliated with the Minority Student Achievement Network (MSAN), in their study of 15 participating urban–suburban school districts—recognized for their academic reputations, well-established economic support of public schools, and location near predominantly White universities—found that Black students performed less well on measures of student achievement (Ferguson, 2002). These researchers demonstrated how even highly touted school districts struggle with serious achievement disparities between Black and White students. One of the major concerns of the MSAN has been the teachers' lower expectations and demands of Black students in comparison to White students. For example, White students were almost twice as likely as Black students to cite teacher demands as motivating them to "work really hard."

Preparing White Educators in the Mixed School Setting

To better prepare White teachers to teach children from diverse backgrounds, as well as to respond to the scarcity of ethnically diverse educators for America's ever-changing public school population, a number of researchers (e.g., Gay, 1997; Irvine, 1990, 1999a, 1999b; Ladson-Billings, 1994) began developing models to effectively prepare pre-service teachers, many of whom were White and middle-class. Recognizing the multiple barriers to recruiting and retaining Black educators, these researchers devised various culturally appropriate ways of teacher preparation, some of which included culturally synchronized teaching and culturally relevant teaching. Given that more than 90 percent of all public school teachers in the United States are White, it makes sense for teacher preparation programs to focus on effectively preparing these prospective teachers to teach children who are socioeconomically and ethnically different from them.

The Recruitment of Black Educators into Mixed Schools

But the preparation of White teachers to teach Black children is not sufficient. If there is a genuine commitment to educationally preparing low-income African American children, policy makers are also going to have to recruit more Black educators. But because pre-service teacher programs at many predominantly White universities have made few strides in recruiting a critical mass of Black teacher candidates, there is a need to consider other possible sources. An untapped source of Black teachers might be Black colleges and universities. Historically and across three of the schools profiled in this book, these colleges have been a significant source of Black educators who worked well with African American children.

In comparison to predominantly White institutions, historically Black colleges and universities (HBCUs) continue to disproportionately prepare Black educators. More than 37 percent of African American educators today received their teacher preparation at HBCUs. Almost half of the African American educators in the South today received their teaching degrees from HBCUs, and these institutions represent two-thirds of all the top-producing colleges and universities of teaching degree recipients who are Black (United Negro College Fund, 2001; Southern Education Foundation, 2003). Yet Black educators are needed more than ever in U.S. public schools, where more than 98 percent of all Black children attend school.

A unique aspect of HBCUs, and the source of their potential today, is that they have disproportionately been committed to educating low-income Black students, many who did not receive adequate preparation in K–12 schools. For example, public HBCUs like Fort Valley State University in Georgia have "catch-up academics," and almost all of these schools have historically reached out to and prepared children who were educationally underprepared prior to college (Willie, Reddick, & Brown, 2006). Although many of these young people did not have stellar scores on standardized tests, HBCUs have given them a chance to attend college.

Moreover, African American children who are reared in poverty are more likely to consider teaching as a first-option profession, much more so than middle-class Black children, whose parents often dissuade them from the teaching profession altogether (Gordon, 2005). A plausible focus of recruitment efforts would be individuals who identify—across race and social class—with the children whom they will teach. The educators who will play a key role in the educational salvation of low-income and urban Black children just may be those who once lived in urban, predominantly low-income African American communities.

To accomplish this, however, teacher accreditation programs would have to move beyond a candidate's score on a test and consider an array of ways to gauge whether an individual is prepared for and committed to teaching low-income African American children. Furthermore, high scores on college admissions tests, teacher preparation programs, and teacher exams do not ensure that the person will be a quality teacher of low-income Black children. Such measures only assist in further reducing the numbers of prospective Black teachers. Just as Black children need educators who are prepared in their particular disciplinary fields, they also need educators who are committed to remaining in the field and to teaching them.

Supporting Black Families in Mixed Schools

Throughout their experiences in the United States, African American families have done a remarkable job of serving as support structures against the constraints imposed on African American people in the broader society. Today, African American families in urban communities must deal with a myriad of issues, such as lack of education, poverty, deindustrialization, and high incarceration and unemployment rates of African American males, all which profoundly affect African American families and contribute to the overwhelming number of one-parent households. Unlike African American families who historically operated in an extended family network, and due to the urbanization of African American people, many of the families described in this book were reliant on the school as a supportive institution for them and their children. Unfortunately, some of the schools could fill this role better than others.

The St. Louis parents whose children attended the magnet school and the predominantly White suburban school needed transportation services in order to get to the schools for special events and meetings. Because of these transportation problems and job schedules, they were not able to get to the schools often. The SHARP program at Spring Hill Elementary allowed the White educators to begin to understand the experiences of their African American students by providing an opportunity for them to visit some of the communities where the children lived. (Unfortunately, though, it was discontinued because of budget cuts.) These are the kinds of culturally affirming and educational programs that predominantly White schools need—whether funded by a desegregation plan or not.

Due to the many challenges and dilemmas facing urban communities and schools, there is an urgent need for support systems for those individuals who remain in urban communities and schools. Realistically, solving the problems of urban communities requires much more than giving financial and political support to a school so as to provide stability and an enriched educational environment. Macro-issues such as joblessness, poor housing, drugs, racism, poverty, and discrimination also adversely impact urban schools and communities.

Some school reform proposals and initiatives have attempted to deal with the array of societal issues facing students, schools, and communities. These reforms (although proposed 10 to 20 years ago) suggest that schools and communities can be the bases from which social services for children and families are provided (Comer, 1980; Crowson & Boyd, 1993; Hale, 2001; Heath & McLaughlin, 1987). One such reform has been the *School Development Program* developed by James Comer (1980, 1987, 1988). This program, based in the school, takes a team approach to enhancing

the educational experiences of children by bringing together professionals such as teachers, social workers, and mental health specialists. This
model is based on the notion that children's home and school experiences
are significant in shaping their opportunities for school success.

EDUCATIONAL REFORM AND POLICY
IN THE TWENTY-FIRST CENTURY

Rather than being driven by sound empirical research that focuses specifically on understanding the factors and conditions that are conducive
to promoting Black children's educational excellence, policy makers have
too often pushed reforms and policies that were politically and ideologically driven rather than educationally sound. Consequently, Black children have become the secondary or incidental beneficiaries of reforms and
policies rather than the primary ones. And in the implementation of these
reforms, the significance of poverty, race, and racism in affecting the conditions in which these children live and attend school is rarely considered.
The 2007 Supreme Court ruling against the use of race to promote public
school desegregation further highlights how the significance of race and
racism have been minimized in the discourse on inequality.

End of an Era? The Supreme Court and
the Racial Balancing of Public Schools

During the summer of 2007, the United States Supreme Court issued a
5–4 ruling striking down two cases (one from Louisville, Kentucky, and
the other from Seattle, Washington) that involved the use of race to promote public school desegregation. In the Louisville school district (which
was approximately 34 percent Black), district leaders wanted to continue
a voluntary desegregation plan that allowed schools to enroll a Black student population between 15 and 50 percent. If a particular school's racial
balance was below the 15 percent Black student enrollment, then the
school could include race as a factor in determining which applicant could
be chosen. Seattle, on the other hand, operated an "open-choice" plan in
which parents could decide which school to send their children to. If there
were more applicants to one particular school than there were spaces
available, the school system wanted to continue to use race as an "integration tie-breaker."

In both cases, White parents whose children were denied admission
to the schools of their choice sued, arguing that the racially balanced
measures were unconstitutional. Their argument was supported by the

Bush administration and the U.S. Department of Education. By ruling against race-conscious policies predicated on improving access to quality education, the Supreme Court ignored the history of race and schooling in the United States—a history that initially denied education to Black people and later deliberately limited Black people's access to quality schooling. Supporters of race-conscious policies, on the other hand, attested to the many benefits of diverse school settings for children's educational and social development.

But would a Court decision in either direction make a major difference in the education of Black children on a day-to-day basis? If the Court had decided that the Louisville and Seattle desegregation plans were permissible, would there be cause for celebration? Neither decision would change the fact that the average twelfth-grade Black student reads at an eighth-grade level. Or that only about half of all Black students in the United States will graduate from high school.[2] Nor would it address the root causes of de facto segregation in U.S. public schools, which include persistent race stigmatizing and segregated housing patterns, caused in part by deeply rooted wealth inequalities between White and Black people in the United States.[3]

Considering the Court's 2007 decision, as well as the varied scholarly findings on the academic benefits of racially desegregated schools for Black children, are genuinely integrated schools realistic educational options for the majority of Black children today? Given U.S. demographic shifts (particularly the increasing Latino student presence in urban areas and the South) and entrenched racial patterns in schools and communities, it is imperative that schools that disproportionately enroll low-income and minority students provide a quality schooling for those children. While scholars may debate the various directions in which the Supreme Court could have gone and the consequences for schooling nationally, Black children's educational futures cannot rest on promises alone. Instead, their educational futures will depend on the collective response of scholars, educators, and activists to the Court's recent and future decisions.

School Choice

Alternative public educational models such as magnet schools and charter schools must go beyond "rescuing a few" to "saving the many." As highlighted in this book, policy proposals such as "school choice" have often been presented as the panacea for the problems that impact urban schools and communities. However, the litmus test for school choice plans is the extent to which these schools serve students from low-income families. In the case of Denson Magnet School, informational and social networks within and outside of the African American parents' community were important in their decision to apply to and enroll their children in the magnet school, a public school choice model. Too often, school choice plans make it very difficult for many low-income parents to make an informed choice. Therefore, when devising parental choice plans, the following question should also be considered: Do low-income African American parents really have a choice in these plans?

As the findings from the multiple ethnographic case studies illustrate, some African Americans are supportive of school choice because they have little confidence in the quality of the schools their children attend. They may not necessarily embrace a conservative perspective on schooling and society. The traditional ideological spectrum in which liberal is to the left and conservative is to the right just does not apply to these parents and their experiences with education. These low-income African American families merely wanted what was best for their children, just as middle-class parents have the ability to provide what is best for their children. But, if these parents choose schools outside of their communities, they will face an array of problems, such as the lack of informational and social networks, time and transportation problems in attending events at the schools, and lack of connectedness to the schools their children attend. These all play a role in the perils that their children experience in these schools.

An increasing number of African American families, often of middle income, are opting out of traditional forms of schools altogether and choosing to home-school their children. African American families decide to home-school their children for numerous reasons. Although some African American families have the resources, time, and confidence to educate their children, such an option is not available to a significant percentage of African American families because of African Americans' disproportionate poverty rate. One of the major critiques of African American families' decisions to home-school is that by doing so the Black middle class abandons public schooling—and thus abandons its communal obligations and consigns low-income African American children to public schools. But in some ways African Americans' decisions to home-school their children is reminiscent of the agency that African Americans have displayed when their children were being denied access to literacy during and after slavery (Anderson, 1978; Williams, 2005).

One thing is certain. Researchers, policy analysts, and educators have to seriously engage the question of how best to guarantee that African American children from low-income families will be provided with high-quality schooling that does not prepare them to reproduce the socioeconomic conditions from which they came but, instead, enables them to develop the requisites to become confident and productive members of

society. Obviously, such an undertaking will have to go beyond just changing the schooling experiences of these children to include changing the
social and economic conditions in which these children's' schooling occurs. It is not enough to talk about how to improve the schooling of Black
children who live in poverty; there needs to be a simultaneous discussion
on how to take these children out of poverty. Short of that, many educational reform efforts will be futile.

CONCLUSION

Efforts to improve urban schools in general and African American education in particular cannot be separated from a serious analysis of historical,
social, political, and economic forces in U.S. society. School quality is inextricably linked to housing, politics, and economics, which makes it in-
cumbent upon grassroots and established leadership to ensure that these
multiple spheres are brought together in the best interest of the students.
The insights presented in this chapter (and book) are of further importance because the fact remains that a great number of low-income African American students will continue to attend urban schools. Devising
effective strategies to ensure equitable schooling for low-income African
American children is paramount to maintaining the integrity and spirit of
Brown.

Finally, it is important to note that many urban schools do not pos-
sess the kinds of organizational structures and processes that two of the
schools, Fairmont and Lincoln, displayed. Nevertheless, findings from these
two schools serve as a source for understanding the role that similarly situated schools might play in educating low-income African American students. Just as the biblical town of Nazareth was considered hopeless, and
yet from this place emerged the one that Moses and the prophets had
written about, who knows what might arise from a careful study of contemporary, urban, and predominantly African American schools and communities that exude agency? One just might find that the solution resides,
as Du Bois said, within the "souls" of Black people. But first, there has to
be the belief that Black people have something of value. Accepting this
scholarly charge is essential, not because one should give up on the hope
of an integrated society or a society in which racial and economic inequalities cease to exist, but because of the need to provide the best schooling
experiences (academically and socioculturally) for those who have been
consigned to society's abyss.

In the end, the educational advancement of African American people
cannot be solely measured by the extent to which some African American

children are able to have a middle-class home and schooling experience—almost in a "talented tenth" sense with the notion that they will reach back to help those at the bottom.[4] Instead, it can be best measured by the extent to which African American children at the bottom are provided the social and educational means to elevate themselves. That is the contemporary educational struggle facing low-income Black children in the urban centers of the United States.

APPENDIX

Methodology

Methodologically, this study of urban African American schooling in St. Louis and Atlanta was situated within a sociohistorical understanding of the respective school districts and cities. The research design drew from a methodological tradition employed by W. E. B. Du Bois (1899, 1902/1978a) in his "community study" of Black community life of Philadelphia. In his seminal work, *The Philadelphia Negro: A Social Study*, Du Bois (1899) was one of the first scholars to study the role of race, class, and social structure in American life and to argue that the study of a group should occur within the particular context in which the group exists (see also Alridge, 2008; Stewart, 1990; Zuberi, 2004).

Du Bois termed his research study—which employed ethnographic research techniques and descriptive statistics—a "social study" because of its in-depth focus on a particular social context. According to Du Bois (1978c) a "'social study' has come to be applied to such investigations as seek to go further and deeper than a national census and study indefinitely and, within limits, exhaustively, the conditions of life and action in certain localities" (p. 67).

The social study method guided the research studies and frames this book. During 1993 and 1994, Fairmont Elementary School and Denson Magnet School were 2 of 26 schools in St. Louis (8 predominantly Black schools, 8 integrated schools, and 10 magnet schools) in which an anonymous survey questionnaire was distributed to all fifth-grade parents and nonadministrative certified staff in each school. The initial phase of the investigation of Fairmont Elementary School, Denson Magnet School, and Spring Hill Elementary Schools was drawn from a multicity (St. Louis, Cincinnati, and Nashville) research study of magnet and neighborhood schools to examine the impact of public school choice on the development and maintenance of school community. The study on school choice was led by Ellen Goldring and Claire Smrekar, both professors at Peabody College of Vanderbilt University. Below, I further describe the research process in St. Louis and Atlanta.

SELECTION AND ETHNOGRAPHIC DATA
COLLECTION IN THE SCHOOLS

I selected Fairmont Elementary School in St. Louis for in-depth investigation after African American educators in the city and the school repeatedly suggested that the school be considered for further study because of its academic reputation and what they defined as a "strong connection" with African American families and the nearby community. Survey data from the multicity study affirmed these educators' assertions about Fairmont. The most frequent response that parents surveyed gave for choosing Fairmont was its proximity to their homes. The second most frequent response was the school's academic reputation. More than 90 percent of the parents surveyed "strongly agreed" or "agreed" that the school created opportunities for parents to be involved. I then chose the other two schools (Denson Magnet School and Spring Hill Elementary School) because they also enrolled students—though not many—from the Fairmont attendance zone. I wanted to know in what ways the St. Louis desegregation plan shaped African American families' relationships with their children's schools.

From 1994 to 1997, I conducted an intensive investigation of Fairmont, Denson, and Spring Hill. Over this 3-year period, I lived in the city for weeks at a time, visiting the schools and the community to conduct interviews and observations. I also attended key events such as Meet-the-Teacher Night, open houses, holiday celebrations (Christmas and Kwanzaa), Black History Month programs (if the school celebrated them), and other events. Afterwards, from 1998 to 2001, I visited the schools once a year, for approximately a week at a time, to examine the change and continuity in the school.

After completing a substantial amount of research in St. Louis, I became interested in developing a broader understanding of the schooling of Black children—but in a context, one in which desegregation was not the district's policy. So the public school system in Atlanta became a new research site shortly after I began a faculty position at the University of Georgia. The Atlanta phase of the research was supported in part by research grants from the Spencer Foundation, the Institute for Behavior Research at the University of Georgia, the Office of the Vice President for Research, and the College of Education at the University of Georgia.

Lincoln Elementary School in Atlanta was purposefully sampled, based on its reputation for playing a key role in the nearby community. In the fall of 1998, a director of an urban educational research project at a local university (Dr. Folami Prescott) initially suggested the school as a possible site. Folami had a strong reputation for her involvement with African

American "grassroots" efforts in Atlanta. Moreover, newspaper articles occasionally featured the school and the principal's accomplishments. In informal conversations with African American residents from the community, many concurred that Lincoln Elementary School maintained a strong relationship with the community. I followed up by seeking additional suggestions from African American educators in the Atlanta public school system, who attributed Lincoln's reputation to the principal, Dr. Frazier. One particular educator, Maude Glanton, was a retired principal from the Atlanta public school system.

An African American female, Dr. Frazier (who unexpectedly passed away in the spring of 1999) was renowned for partnering the school with businesses and community-based agencies.[1] In addition, Lincoln was one of 11 elementary schools in 1997 selected as a "Georgia School of Excellence," based on a combination of factors that included student attendance rates and standardized test scores, the curriculum, and parent participation rates.

My time at Lincoln Elementary spanned the summer of 1999 through the spring of 2002. I lived in the Atlanta metropolitan area, about 20 minutes from the school. I spent the summer and fall of 1999 primarily in the community (twice a week), collecting data and developing rapport with school personnel. During the spring and fall of 2000, I was in the school 3 to 4 days a week observing key events and conducting interviews. In the spring of 2001, I spent approximately 2 days a week in the school and community. In the spring of 2002, I concluded interviews with staff and faculty. Over the course of the research project at Lincoln, I observed Grandparent's Day, Kwanzaa programs, Black History Month programs, and field day. Moreover, I read a book to a fifth-grade class during the Male–Female Read-In sponsored by the school's corporate sponsor, facilitated a seminar on African American education for school personnel, served as an external reviewer for the school's 2001 Student Achievement Plan, and gave the keynote speech at the annual Men's Night Out program that was organized by Dr. Obasi, the guidance counselor.

Ethnographic data collection methods included observations of faculty and staff's interactions with students and families; participant observation; community observations; recording of field notes; informal questioning of community residents; and interviews with parents, residents, and school personnel (Fetterman, 1989; Noblit & Hare, 1988). In addition, documents (brochures, letters, newsletters, handbooks, and information sent home to parents) were collected and analyzed. Archival data provided historical information on each community and school, and U.S. census data (from 1990 and 2000) provided demographic information about the communities.

Observations in all schools and communities uncovered the nature of the relationships between the families and school personnel, as well as how the organizational structures of the schools influenced these relationships. I used a semistructured interview protocol, which enabled the participants to discuss issues beyond the parameters of the study, organized interviews and transcripts by participants' functions and titles, and then coded. The interviews focused on the following: (1) the schools' support for parents and students, (2) parents' roles in the schools, and (3) participants' perceptions of how social forces influenced the nature of the relationships.

More than 75 formal interviews occurred in both cities. In all of the schools, I interviewed fourth- and fifth-grade parents because I wanted to gather information from parents and guardians who could speak definitively about the schools, and these parents were more likely to have had an extended relationship with the school. The educators were randomly selected to ensure a stratified sample as much as possible. Those interviewed reflected the predominant racial and gender composition within each school. Most interviews lasted an hour to an hour and a half; some lasted longer. With the exception of one, the educators were interviewed at school. Most of the Fairmont parents were interviewed at their homes, and many of the Lincoln parents were interviewed at the school or the community program. Mrs. Wright, a Lincoln parent, assisted in securing the Lincoln interviews.

Data analysis focused on the overarching research question and was meta-ethnographic in nature (Noblit & Hare, 1988). The data analysis proceeded in three phases. Phase I involved an analysis of Fairmont Elementary School within the context of the St. Louis desegregation plan; this analysis was comparative in nature and included a magnet school and a predominantly White county school that also enrolled African American students from the community near Fairmont (Morris, 1997). The St. Louis analysis focused on (1) Black parents' reasons for choosing a particular school, (2) the relationships between the schools and Black families, (3) Black students' experiences in each school, and (4) the transfer plan's impact on the relationship between schools and families.

Another researcher—Bob Saffold, a White male and a graduate student at Vanderbilt University—assisted in collecting some of the data at Fairmont Elementary School between 1994 and 1995. Bob reviewed and shared field notes and coded some of the data. Phase II specifically focused on Lincoln Elementary School, and two African American female research assistants assisted in data collection and analysis. In this phase, transitions within the school and community emerged as a major theme from the coding of interview and observational data. Phase III was a cross-case comparison between Fairmont and Lincoln. Research assistants and I reviewed the field notes on each school, searching for overarching themes. We then examined interview transcripts, searching for themes that resonated with and diverged from our field notes. Pattern coding was used to understand participants' continuous patterns of thought, action, and behavior (Fetterman, 1989; Miles & Huberman, 1984; Yin, 1989). The coded Lincoln data were compared with the coded Fairmont data. These data were triangulated with archival data and census data.

Overarching themes and categories emerged, illustrating similarities and dissimilarities between each school and community. The constant comparative method was used to interpret the meaning of the data by developing categories, themes, properties, and tentative hypotheses based on the data from the two schools and communities (Glaser & Strauss, 1967). The findings at both sites were synthesized. Within this synthesis, however, each case maintained its uniqueness and wholeness (Noblit & Hare, 1988). For example, the analysis revealed how participants' experiences and racial discourses were shaped by the different regional contexts, overarching educational policies (e.g., desegregation and accountability), and changes within the schools and communities.

Often, there is the preference for a research design that compares a school that works with one that is failing. I intentionally avoided this when choosing the predominantly African American schools in Atlanta and St. Louis. Due to the overwhelming number of research studies that have focused on failing urban schools, Black parents, and students, I believe that it is also important to investigate schools that successfully educate students—particularly those that disproportionately serve low-income African American students. I already know too much about what is wrong; I wanted to find out about what is right by describing "health" rather than pathology, as Lightfoot (1983) noted.

In qualitative research, the researcher is the primary instrument of data collection (Merriam, 1988). Researchers' identities are essential components of the entire research process (Scheurich & Young, 1997). One cannot discount the race, social class, or political views of the researcher because researchers bring their own epistemological perspectives—ways of knowing—into the framing of researchable questions, data collection and analysis, and interpretations and conclusions. Rather than minimize this influence, I used my racial identity as an interactional quality to glean theoretical perspectives.

For example, the African American educators that I interviewed were extremely eager to discuss how race and racism affected the implementation of the desegregation plan in St. Louis. I have come to believe that my focus on how the plan affected African American education, as well as my racial identity as African American, enhanced my securing the interviews and contributed to the African American educators' comfort and willingness to discuss sensitive issues regarding race. On several occasions, I was invited into administrators' offices and teachers' classrooms to talk for hours after school had ended. In one instance, I went to a teacher's home and talked with her and her husband until about 2 A.M. about her experiences as an African American teacher in St. Louis, the community work that they both were involved with, and larger issues surrounding the St. Louis desegregation plan. The Black respondents trusted and wanted me to hear their views. They seemed to recognize me as one of their own—not only in racial ways but also in terms of a shared socioeconomic background. I spent time in their schools, communities, and in some of their homes, often talking about my experiences attending all-Black schools and growing up during the 1970s and 1980s in public housing in Birmingham, Alabama. These informal conversations seemed to relax them, build trust, and serve as an entrée into other issues of race and social class.

From my experiences with the African American educators in the schools and the residents of the predominantly African American communities, I assert the following: *There is a great need for researchers who presently live in or once lived in urban and predominantly African American communities to conduct empirical investigations of the families, schools, and communities in these places.* Presently, investigations of urban and low-income African American families, communities, and schools are overwhelmingly led by researchers who are familiar with these areas only in academic ways, not in "lived ways." When a researcher lives in or has lived in a community, he or she most likely understands the area at multiple levels: statistically, sociologically, culturally, and personally. There is no debate between etic or emic, only the reconciling of the two.

On the other hand, there are instances in which the researcher's race can make research participants reluctant to talk about their experiences. Scholars have written about African Americans' reluctance to talk candidly with White researchers about their experiences. However, as an African American male, I encountered instances in which it appeared that the White participants would not actually tell me their true feelings about the desegregation plan in St. Louis. This was especially true of the educators at Denson Magnet School, where the desegregation plan was a very sensitive issue.

However, in the predominantly White and suburban school, Spring Hill, the White educators were very open about sharing their perspectives. This was particularly true of the principal, Dr. Tolliver. Thus, being outsiders to the St. Louis public school system might have provided these White educators at Spring Hill with a certain degree of reassurance that there would not be repercussions to their expressed feelings about race and the desegregation plan. One thing to glean from this observation of the participants' responses is that race is ever-present in the research project and needs to be understood even at the level of the interactions between the participants and the researchers. These interactions shape the data collection, analyses, and interpretation—and eventually the write-up of the findings.

In Chapter 6, I presented excerpts from conversations over more than a decade with the Wooden family of St. Louis. During every visit to the city, I explained to the family that I was still working on "that book" that I had told them about at our first meeting.

In Chapter 8, I synthesize the book's major themes and their implications for theory, policy, and practice, with the intent to engage policy makers and academics, as well as school leaders and parents, in thinking critically about the education of African American children. Contemporary scholars consider such an approach to be "critical ethnography" because of its focus on moving beyond just describing "what is" to empowering local communities to generate practices and policies that effectively respond to the issues raised in the research (see, e.g., Foley, 2002; Jordan & Yeomans, 1995; Segall, 2001). Indeed, W. E. B. Du Bois (1898/1978b) asserted that rigorous scholarly investigations of Black people are necessary for generating a conceptual understanding of how to create effective social and educational policies and practices.[2]

Notes

INTRODUCTION

1. The most noted examples of this framework within the past few years have been the following books: *Stepping Over the Color Line* (Wells & Crain, 1997), *Savage Inequalities* (Kozol, 1991), *The Shame of the Nation* (Kozol, 2005), *Ghetto Schooling* (Anyon, 1997), and a number of edited books, including *Dismantling Desegregation* (Orfield & Eaton, the Harvard Project on School Desegregation, 1996), *School Resegregation* (Boger & Orfield, 2005), and *Lessons in Integration* (Frankenberg & Orfield, 2007).

2. For other insightful critiques regarding this one-dimensional representation of *Brown*, see Crenshaw (1988), Dougherty (2004), and Ladson-Billings (2004).

3. In *Black Visions: The Roots of Contemporary African-American Political Ideologies*, Michael Dawson (2001) describes six political ideologies that characterize the contours of Black political thought in America: radical egalitarianism, disillusioned liberalism, Black Marxism, Black conservatism, Black feminism, and Black nationalism. The push for integrated schooling is more aligned with the radical egalitarian political thought.

4. Black communities began experiencing gentrification during the late 1990s. The implications for the schools and communities will be highlighted in Chapter 8.

5. A number of scholarly books in educational history have critiqued the one-dimensional view of African Americans' educational quest as a desire primarily for integrated schooling and highlighted the edifying role of all-Black schools (albeit legally segregated ones) for African American students and communities. For further reading, see Cecelski (1994), Siddle Walker (1996), Dougherty (2004), and Morris and Morris (2002).

CHAPTER 1

1. For example, at the time in which the research in these schools was taking place, the following cities had a Black student population that exceeded 80 percent of the total public school population: Atlanta, Georgia (89 percent); Baltimore, Maryland (88 percent); Birmingham, Alabama (96 percent); Detroit,

Michigan (90 percent); Jackson, Mississippi (95 percent); Memphis, Tennessee (86 percent); Richmond, Virginia (90 percent); and St. Louis, Missouri (80 percent). (U.S. Department of Education 2001–2002). Since then, the Black student population percentage has decreased in some of these cities, but many are still more than 75 to 80 percent African American. By 2008, and as a result of a number of factors that are discussed later, the above cities decreased to the following percentages of African American: Atlanta, Georgia (78 percent), Baltimore, Maryland (75 percent), Birmingham, Alabama (87 percent), Detroit, Michigan (85 percent), Jackson, Mississippi (81 percent), Memphis, Tennessee (75 percent), Richmond, Virginia (77 percent). The percentage of Black students in St. Louis, Missouri, remained the same (80 percent). (U.S. Department of Education, 2008).

2. For other insightful critiques regarding this one-dimensional representation of Brown, see Crenshaw (1988), Dougherty (2004), and Ladson-Billings (2004).

3. The notion that integration characterized Black people's quest for quality schooling is more aligned with the radical egalitarian political thought addressed by Dawson.

4. For more on Malcolm X's Black nationalist thought and the schooling of Black children, see Morris (2001).

5. Du Bois's ideology was not static; but changed from advocating integration to embracing an ideology that suggested Black survival through Black self-help and voluntary segregation: "But of course, no idea is perfect and forever valid. Always to be living and apposite and timely, it must be modified and adapted to changing facts" (Du Bois, 1986a/1940, p. 776). For a cogent articulation of Du Bois's educational thought, see Alridge's (2008).

6. Wells and Crain (1997) particularly noted the successes that some of these Black students experienced in the predominantly White schools in the suburbs. Conversely, they primarily highlighted the academic and social problems of those Black students who remained in their Black schools and decided not to transfer into the predominantly White suburban schools.

7. See Hurston (1955).

8. This statement was given by King at a speech in Montgomery, Alabama, in 1959 and quoted in Freeman (2004).

9. Bell is also one of the progenitors of critical race theory (CRT). The interest convergence dilemma posited by Bell (1980) results in Whites rather than Blacks being the primary beneficiaries of civil rights legislation. Examples of such legislation predicated on improving the conditions of African Americans include desegregation plans that have often involved the disproportionate busing of African Americans into predominantly White schools and the creation of well-funded magnet schools to lure White students back into urban schools, as well as affirmative action hiring policies in which the major beneficiaries have been White women. For more on CRT and education, see Dixson &Bousseau, 2006; Duncan, 2002; Tate, 1997.

10. South St. Louis was once a predominantly White community where the predominantly White schools were located. During the 1950s, the St. Louis Board of Education tried to relieve overcrowding in the schools by busing Black children to White schools on the south side. These students were in the school on

different schedules and in different classrooms. The north side is where African Americans primarily lived and went to school.

CHAPTER 2

1. After World War II, many American families also became beneficiaries of the GI Bill, which provided educational opportunities for returning soldiers as well as housing policies that enabled large numbers of families (particularly White families) to leave impoverished homes and move into the working and middle class. Although some African Americans also benefited from the GI Bill, they often were discriminated against in terms of receiving benefits.

2. For a thorough discussion on the White business elite's complicity in the demise of urban school systems that had became predominantly Black during the 1960s and 1970s, see Henig, Hula, Orr, and Pedescleaux (1999). In this book, the authors challenged the notion that Black-led cities would result in tangible educational benefits for African Americans, particularly those who were poor. They proposed that this thesis was not true because although African Americans gained political power, they still lacked economic power, which overwhelmingly resided in the hands of Whites.

3. Deirdre Royster (2003) shows the inequitable opportunities that Black men face when seeking blue-collar jobs. Through detailed ethnographic research, Royster challenges the notion that race is insignificant in the securing of working-class jobs by highlighting how White supervisors and foremen engage in invisible practices that disadvantage Black men and advantage White men.

4. While facility inequality does not convey the complete story of the consequences of segregation, the systematic denial of equal educational resources to Black people further perpetuated notions of Black inferiority. Still, even though resources and facilities were lacking, many Black educators cared deeply about Black children.

5. The U.S. government sets the poverty line based on what it costs families to have the beginnings of the basic necessities of modern American life such as food, shelter, clothing, health care, and transportation. Each year, the federal government calculates the minimum amount of money required by families to meet these basic needs. The resulting calculation is what is commonly referred to as the "poverty line." For 2003, the government had set the poverty guidelines for a family of four at $18,810 (U.S. Census Bureau, 2004b).

CHAPTER 3

1. For example, in a study of African American adolescents in a suburban context, I found out that many of the African American parents believe that the district's theme schools are the same as magnet schools. The superintendent noted that there is no difference between the regular public schools and the theme

schools but that many parents considered the theme schools to be the same as magnet schools.

2. VICC's purpose was threefold: (1) to administer the student transfer and teacher exchange component of the settlement agreement; (2) to provide staff development opportunities; and (3) to oversee student transportation. The council was comprised of one representative from each participating school district, the *Liddell* plaintiffs, the NAACP, and the State of Missouri.

3. Title I is a compensatory program designed to improve the academic achievement of students from low-income backgrounds. The Elementary and Secondary Education Act of 1965 authorized funds for elementary and secondary schools. The act has been authorized every five years; the most recent authorization of it has been the No Child Left Behind Act of 2001.

4. For a discussion of how social class influences access to education, see Rothstein (2004).

5. For an in-depth discussion of social capital theory, see Bourdieu (1986), Coleman (1987, 1988), and Dika and Singh (2002). Embracing Coleman's view of social capital as positive social control based on trust and information channels, a number of scholars over the past decade have suggested that low-income communities might generate social capital when families, communities, and schools work together in the interest of students (see Cibulka & Kritek, 1996).

6. Furthermore, class status for African Americans is ambiguous, especially when compared to White Americans; one might be middle-class based on status rather than income (see also Pattillo-McCoy, 1999).

7. These two African American parents were not residents of the 'Ville and thus not part of the larger study. They were informally interviewed during the time that I spent at the school.

8. Patricia Hill-Collins (2000, 2004) notes the divergent ways in which Black women are portrayed in U.S. society: Poor Black women are stereotyped as welfare queens, lazy and shiftless, while middle-class Black women are considered "bitches" because of their independent nature.

9. African languages might include Twi, Ibo, Yoruba, or Kiswahili.

10. Ramadan is an Islamic holiday that usually occurs in the autumn.

11. For more on this topic, see Lee, Menkart, and Okazawa-Rey (1998), which provides educators with practical tools for deconstructing surface-level celebrations and analyses of culture in schools and societies.

12. It is possible that my identity as an African American male researcher had something to do with their reluctance. As a scholarly community, we generally need more research studies that pay greater attention to the researcher's identity and how it shapes the overall research process. Then again, I had very candid interviews with the White teachers in the predominantly White suburban school that I profile later.

CHAPTER 4

1. Dr. Tolliver resigned from Spring Hill Elementary School during the summer of 1996 to became the principal in another county school district. The secre-

tary, Mrs. Anderson, said that Dr. Tolliver had been seeking a position in the central office in the Homewood School District but was passed over. She said that the district to which he went had been recruiting him for the past 3 years.

2. Rastafarians are followers of Haile Selassie, the former emperor of Ethiopia. The prime belief of the Rastafarians is that Haile Selassie was god on earth. They usually wear dreadlocks, a manner in which the person's hair is allowed to grow until it begins to form locks. However, everyone that wears dreadlocks is not Rastafarian; some people wear their hair like this as a matter of style.

3. Born in 1887 in Jamaica, Marcus Garvey moved to the United States in 1916 and began chapters of the organization he founded, the Universal Negro Improvement Association (UNIA). He proposed a "Back to Africa" movement for African Americans. Marcus Garvey was later deported from the United States on accusations of mail fraud and died in London in 1940.

4. See Goldring and Smrekar (1995).

5. Although I interviewed these African American parents informally in the hallway, I did not conduct in-depth interviews with them. Methodologically, I focused specifically on those African American parents who lived within the attendance zone of the predominantly African American neighborhood school in the city. I wanted to look at African American parents' experiences in Spring Hill in comparison to the experiences of parents at Fairmont Elementary School.

CHAPTER 5

1. This larger study was part of a Spencer Foundation funded research study led by Ellen Goldring and Claire Smrekar at Vanderbilt University.

2. Over this 3-year period, I lived in the city for weeks at a time, visiting the schools and the community to conduct interviews and observations. I also attended key events, such as Meet-the-Teacher Night, open houses, holiday celebrations (Christmas and Kwanzaa), Black History Month programs (if the school celebrated them), and other events. Afterwards, from 1998 to 2001, I visited the schools once a year, for approximately a week at a time, to examine the change and continuity in the respective schools. After completing a substantial amount of research (data collection and analysis) in St. Louis, I became interested in developing a broader understanding of the schooling of Black children—but in a different context, one in which desegregation was not the district's policy.

3. The Atlanta phase of the research was supported in part by research grants from the Spencer Foundation, the Institute for Behavior Research at the University of Georgia, and the College of Education at the University of Georgia.

4. Test score data were not available for Lincoln Elementary School students during the 2002–2003 academic year. Therefore, I used the 2004–2005 academic year to give the reader three years of test score data.

5. Data from the 1990 census revealed that 37 percent (tract 1) and 47 percent (tract 2) of the families lived below the poverty level. Racial demographic changes in the community were most evident in census tract 1, where the White population increased from 3 percent in 1990 to almost 8 percent in 2000.

6. The Black teachers' ethnic diversity at Lincoln Elementary is a microcosm of the growth of the foreign-born Black population in the U.S. South, particularly in Atlanta. For example, from 1990 to 2000, metropolitan Atlanta's West Indian population increased from 8,342 to 35,308, representing a 323.3% growth over the decade. Over this same period, the area's African population increased from 8918 individuals to 34,302, representing a 284% increase over the decade (Logan & Deane, 2003; U.S. Census Bureau, 1990, 2000).

7. In many parts of the United States, Black and White children just do not attend schools together. Some of this is attributed to the dismantling of desegregation, to the fact that many Black people cannot afford to live in communities that are predominantly White, and to the fact that many White people refuse to live in communities that have a significant Black population. Historical housing patterns have created entrenched housing inequities in the United States that become perpetuated.

CHAPTER 6

1. The Great Black Migration of the early to mid-20th century and the Second Great Black Migration, which lasted from 1941 to 1970, witnessed a mass exodus of Black people out of the rural South to northern and midwestern states in search of greater political, social, and economic "promised lands" (Arnesen, 2002; Davis & Donaldson, 1975; Farley & Allen, 1987; Lemann, 1991).

CHAPTER 7

1. M. Carl Holman was an African American poet, playwright, and author. He is best known for *The Baptizin*. He graduated from Lincoln University in Missouri and later received master's degrees from the University of Chicago and Yale University. He taught English at Clark College in Atlanta (which later became Clark Atlanta University) for 14 years, Hampton University, and Lincoln University. Mr. Holman served as the deputy director of the Civil Rights Commission in 1966 and as the director of the National Urban Coalition from 1971 to 1988.

CHAPTER 8

1. An overarching assumption of recent housing policies such as HOPE VI is that low-income families in highly concentrated impoverished communities will have greater access to social capital if the poverty in these communities becomes deconcentrated. Formally known as the Urban Revitalization Demonstration Project, HOPE VI is a product of the U.S. Congress and the Department of Housing and Urban Development (HUD); it is an attempt to transform distressed public housing by reducing the amount of concentrated poverty in a particular locale.

Specifically, HOPE VI is premised on the notion that if low-income families lived in more middle-class and less racially segregated communities and schools, then these children would benefit from the capital within these communities and schools. Theories of social and cultural capital inform HOPE VI because there is the presumption that African American children, by attending schools in less impoverished and less racially segregated communities, will then have access to better informational networks.

2. The situation is even worse for Black students in some states such as Georgia, where only 46 percent who begin ninth grade will graduate from high school 4years later.

3. According to the Pew Wealth Study, the median net wealth of African Americans is $6,000, compared to the median net wealth of White households, which is $88,000. According to William Darity, a professor of African American Studies and Economics at Duke University, "if African Americans saved all of their income (for a decade)—that is, if we didn't eat, pay any bills, but saved every cent of income—we could not close the wealth gap." See "Wealth of a White Nation: Blacks Sink Deeper in Hole," at http://www.blackcommentator .com/110/110_cover_white_wealth.htm.

4. W. E. B. Du Bois is well known for espousing a philosophy of the "talented tenth," in which a select group of Black youth/people would become college educated and then this group would serve as the vanguard for the majority of Black people (Du Bois, 1903/1986b). Later, Du Bois became disillusioned with the ability of this group to elevate the masses because of its preoccupation with elevating itself and its desire to distance itself from the masses—proximally and psychologically. Du Bois concluded that middle-class Black people often forgo the racial uplift component in order to maintain their middle-class status or to move into a higher-class status. Consequently, Du Bois later proposed a notion called the "guiding one-hundredth," in which the premise was that the entire community of Black people—poor folks included—would become educated and lead the group (Du Bois, 1948/1996).

APPENDIX

1. By telephone, Dr. Frazier expressed interest in the research project. Unfortunately, we never met. The new principal, an African American woman (Mrs. Jones), made the decision to allow the school to serve as a research site.

2. For more on Du Bois's view of the role of social science research, see *W. E. B. Du Bois: On Sociology and the Black Community* (edited by Green & Driver, 1978).

References

Alexander, K. L., Entwisle, D. R., & Thompson, M. S. (1987). School performance, status relations, and the structure of sentiment: Bringing the teacher back in. *American Sociology Review, 52*, 665–682.

Alridge, D. P. (2002, April). *W.E.B. Du Bois and the separate Black school and integrated school dichotomy/paradox.* Paper presented at the annual meeting of the American Educational Research Association, New Orleans.

Alridge, D. P. (2003). The dilemmas, challenges, and duality of an African American educational historian. *Educational Researcher, 32*(9), 25–34.

Alridge, D.P. (2008). *The educational thought of W.E.B. Du Bois: An intellectual history.* New York: Teachers College Press.

Amos v. Board of Directors of the City of Milwaukee, 408 F. Supp. 765 (1976).

Anderson, E. (1978). *A place on the corner.* Chicago: University of Chicago Press.

Anderson, E. (1990). *Streetwise: Race, class, and change in an urban community.* Chicago: University of Chicago Press.

Anderson, E. (1999). *Code of the street: Decency, violence, and the moral life of the inner city.* New York: Norton.

Anderson, J. D. (1988). *The education of Blacks in the South, 1860–1935.* Chapel Hill: University of North Carolina Press.

Anyon, J. (1997). *Ghetto schooling: A political economy of urban educational reform.* New York: Teachers College Press.

Arnesen, E. (2002). *Black protest and the great migration: A brief history with documents.* Boston: Bedford/St. Martin's.

Arthur v. Nyquist, 415 F. Supp. 904 (1976).

Asante, M. K. (1987). *The Afrocentric idea.* Philadelphia: Temple University Press.

Banks, J. A. (1993). The canon debate, knowledge construction, and multicultural education. *Educational Researcher, 33*(5), 4–14.

Bayor, R. H. (1996). *Race and the shaping of twentieth-century Atlanta.* Chapel Hill: University of North Carolina Press.

Beauboeuf-La Fontant, T. (1999). A movement against and beyond boundaries: "Politically relevant teaching" among African American teachers. *Teachers College Record, 100*(4), 702–723.

Bell, D. A. (1980). *Brown v. Board of Education* and the interest-convergence dilemma. *Harvard Law Review, 93*, 518–533.

Bell, D. A. (1987). *And we are not saved: The elusive quest for racial justice.* New York: Basic Books.

Bell, D. A. (1992). *Faces at the bottom of the well: The permanence of racism*. New York: Basic Books.

Bell, D. A. (2000). *Race, racism and American law* (4th ed.). Gaithersburg, MD: Aspen.

Bell, D. A. (2004). *Silent covenants: Brown v. Board of Education and the unfulfilled hopes for racial reform*. New York: Oxford University Press.

Benham, M. K. P. (1997). Silences and serenades: The journeys of three ethnic minority women school leaders. *Anthropology & Education Quarterly, 28*(2), 280–307.

Billingsley, A. (1968). *Black families in White America*. Englewood Cliffs, NJ: Prentice Hall.

Billingsley, A. (1992). *Climbing Jacob's ladder: The enduring legacy of African American families*. New York: Simon & Schuster.

Boger, C., & Orfield, G. (Eds.). (2005). *School resegregation: Must the South turn back?* Chapel Hill, NC: Univesity of North Carolina Press.

Bourdieu, P. (1986). The forms of capital. In J. Richardson (Ed.), *Handbook of theory and research for the sociology of education* (pp. 241–258). Westport, CT: Greenwood.

Boykin, A. W. (1994). Harvesting culture and talent: African American children and school reform. In R. Rossi (Ed.), *Schools and students at risk: Context and framework for positive change* (pp. 116–138). New York: Teachers College Press.

Braddock, J. H. (1989). *Tracking: Implications for African American students*. Baltimore, MD: Johns Hopkins University, Center for Research on Effective Schooling for Disadvantaged Students.

Brown v. Board of Education of Topeka, Kansas, 347 U.S. 483 (1954).

Carter, P. (2005). *Keepin' it real: School success beyond Black and White*. New York: Oxford University Press.

Carter, R. L. (1996). The unending struggle for equal educational opportunity. In E. C. Lagemann & L. P. Miller (Eds.), Brown v. Board: *The challenge for today's schools* (pp. 19–26). New York: Teachers College Press.

Casey, K. (1993). *I answer with my life*. New York: Routledge & Kegan Paul.

Cecelski, D. S. (1994). *Along freedom road: Hyde County North Carolina and the fate of Black schools in the South*. Chapel Hill: University of North Carolina Press.

Cibulka, J. G., & Kritek, W. J. (Eds.). (1996). *Coordination among schools, families, and communities: Prospects for educational reform*. Albany, NY: State University of New York Press.

Citizens' Commission on Civil Rights. (1997). *Difficult choices: Do magnet schools serve children in need?* Washington, DC: Author.

Coleman, J. (1987). Families and schools. *Educational Researcher, 16*(6), 32–38.

Coleman, J. (1988). Social capital and the creation of human capital. *American Journal of Sociology, 94*, 95–120.

Comer, J. P. (1980). *School power: Implications of an intervention project*. New York: Free Press.

Comer, J. P. (1987). New Haven's School-Community Connection, *Educational Leadership, 44*, 13–16.

Comer, J. P. (1988, November). Educating poor minority children. *Scientific American, 259*(5), 42–48.

Cone, J. H. (1990). *A Black theology of liberation* (20th anniversary ed.). Maryknoll, NY: Orbis. (Original work published 1970)

Cone, J. H. (1991). *The spirituals and the blues: An interdisciplinary.* Maryknoll, NY: Orbis.

Crenshaw, K. (1988). Race, reform, and retrenchment: Transformation and legitimation in antidiscrimination law. *Harvard Law Review, 101,* 1331–1387.

Cross, W. E. (1991). *Shades of Black: Diversity in African-American identity.* Philadelphia: Temple University Press.

Crowson, R. L., & Boyd, W. L. (1993). Coordinated services for children: Designing arks for storms and seas unknown. *American Journal of Education, 101,* 140–179.

Darling-Hammond, L., Wise, A. E., & Klein, S. P. (1995). *A license to teach: Building a profession for twenty-first century schools.* Boulder, CO: Westview.

Davis, G. A., & Donaldson, O. F. (1975). *Blacks in the United States: A geographic perspective.* Boston: Houghton Mifflin.

Dawson, M. C. (2001). *Black visions: The roots of contemporary African-American political ideologies.* Chicago: University of Chicago Press.

Dee, T. S. (2001). *Teachers, race and student achievement in a randomized experiment.* Working Paper 8432. Cambridge, MA: National Bureau of Economic Research.

Delpit, L. (1995). *Other people's children: Cultural conflict in the classroom.* New Press.

Dempsey, V., & Noblit, G. (1993). The demise of caring in an African American community: One consequence of school desegregation. *Urban Review, 25*(1), 47–61.

Dika, S. L., & Singh, K. (2002). Applications of social capital in educational literature: A critical synthesis. *Review of Educational Research, 72*(1), 31–60.

Dillard, C. B. (1995). Leading with her life: An African American feminist (re)interpretation of leadership for an urban high school principal. *Educational Administration Quarterly, 31*(4), 539–563.

Dillard, C. B. (2000). The substance of things hoped for, the evidence of things not seen: Examining an endarkened feminist epistemology in educational research and leadership. *International Journal of Qualitative Studies in Education, 13*(6), 661–681.

Dixson, A. D., & Rousseau, C. K. (Eds.). (2006). *Critical race theory in education: All God's children got a song.* New York: Routledge.

Dougherty, J. (2004). *More than one struggle: The evolution of Black school reform in Milwaukee.* Chapel Hill: University of North Carolina Press.

Drake, S., & Cayton, H. R. (1945). *Black metropolis: A study of Negro life in a northern city.* Chicago: University of Chicago Press.

Du Bois, W. E. B. (1899). *The Philadelphia Negro: A social study.* Philadelphia: University of Pennsylvania Press.

Du Bois, W. E. B. (1935). Does the Negro need separate schools? *Journal of Negro Education, 4*(3), 328–335.

Du Bois, W. E. B. (1978a). The Negroes of Dougherty County, Virginia. In D. S. Green & E. D. Driver (Eds.), *W. E. B. Du Bois: On sociology and the Black community* (pp. 154–164). Chicago: University of Chicago Press. (Original work published 1902)

Du Bois, W. E. B. (1978b). The study of the Negro problem. In D. S. Green &
E. D. Driver (Eds.), *W. E. B. Du Bois: On Sociology and the Black community*
(pp. 70–84). Chicago: University of Chicago Press. (Original work published
1898)

Du Bois, W. E. B. (1978c). The twelfth census and the Negro problems. In D. S.
Green & E. D. Driver (Eds.), *W. E. B. Du Bois: On sociology and the Black community* (pp. 65–69). Chicago: University of Chicago Press. (Original work published 1900)

Du Bois, W. E. B. (1986a/1940). *Dusk of dawn: An essay toward an autobiography of
a race concept.* New York: Literary Classics of the United States. (Original work
published 1940)

Du Bois, W. E. B. (1986b). The talented tenth. In N. Huggins (Ed.), *W. E. B. Du
Bois: Writings: The suppression of the African slave trade, The souls of Black folk,
Dusk of dawn, Essays and articles* (pp. 842–861). New York: Literary Classics of
the United States. (Original work published 1903)

Du Bois, W. E. B. (1994). *The souls of Black folk.* New York: Dover. (Original work
published 1903).

Du Bois, W. E. B. (1996). The talented tenth memorial address. In H. L. Gates &
C. West (Eds.). (1984). *W. E. B. Du Bois: Dusk of dawn: An essay toward an autobiography of a race concept.* London: Transaction. (Original work published 1948)

Dudziak, M. (2000). *Cold war civil rights: Race and the image of American democracy.*
Princeton, NJ: Princeton University Press.

Duncan, G. A. (2002). Critical race theory and method: Rendering race in urban
ethnographic research. *Qualitative Inquiry, 8*(1), 85–104.

Dyson. M. E. (1996). *Race rules: Navigating the color line.* Reading, MA: Addison-
Wesley.

Edwards, P. A. (1996). Before and after school desegregation: African American
parents' involvement in schools. In M. Shujaa (Ed.), *Beyond desegregation: The
politics of quality in African American schooling* (pp. 138–161). Thousand Oaks,
CA: Corwin.

Epstein, J. L. (1986). Parents' reactions to teacher practices of parent involvement.
Elementary School Journal, 86, 27–94.

Epstein, J. L. (1992). School and family partnerships. In *Encyclopedia of educational
research* (6th ed., pp. 1139–1151).

Etheridge, S. B. (1979). Impact of the 1954 *Brown vs. Topeka Board of Education* decision on Black educators. *The Negro Educational Review, 30*(4), 217–
232.

Farley, R., & Allen, W. (1987). *The color line and the quality of life in America.* New
York: Russell Sage Foundation.

Ferguson, A. (2000). *Bad boys: Public schools in the making of Black masculinity.* Ann
Arbor: University of Michigan Press.

Ferguson, R. F. (1998a). Teachers' perceptions and expectations and the black-
white test score gap. In C. Jencks & M. Phillips (Eds.), *The black-white test score
gap* (pp. 273–317). Washington, DC: Brookings Institution.

Ferguson, R. F. (1998b). Can schools narrow the test score gap? Teachers' perceptions & expectations and the black-white test score gap. In C. Jencks &

M. Phillips (Eds.), *The black-white test score gap* (pp. 318–374). Washington, DC: Brookings Institution.

Ferguson, R. F. (2002). *Ed-excel assessment of secondary school student culture tabulations by school district and race/ethnicity: Responses from middle school, junior high and high school (2000–2001 school year).* Cambridge, MA: Wiener Center for Social Policy, John F. Kennedy School for Government, Harvard University.

Fetterman, D. M. (1989). *Ethnography step by step.* Newbury Park, CA: Sage.

Foley, D. E. (2002). Critical ethnography: The reflexive turn. *Qualitative Studies, 15*(5), 469–490.

Ford, D. Y., & Harris, J. J., III. (1999). *Multicultural gifted education.* New York: Teachers College Press.

Fordham, S. (1996). *Blacked out: Dilemmas of race, identity, and success at Capital High.* Chicago: University of Chicago Press.

Foster, M. (1990). The politics of race: Through African American teachers' eyes. *Journal of Education, 172*(3), 123–141.

Foster, M. (1995). African American teachers and culturally relevant pedagogy. In J. A. Banks & C. A. M. Banks (Eds.), *Handbook of research on multicultural education* (pp. 570–581). New York: Macmillan.

Foster, M. (1997). *Black teachers on teaching.* New York: New Press.

Frankenberg, E., & Orfield, G. (Eds.). (2007). *Lessons in integration: Realizing the promise of racial diversity in American schools.* Charlottesville: University of Virginia Press.

Franklin, V. P. (1990). "They rose and fell together": African American educators and community leadership, 1795–1954. *Journal of Education, 172*(3), 39–64.

Frazier, E. F. (1939). *The Negro family in the United States.* Chicago: University of Chicago Press.

Frazier, E. F. (1957). *The Black bourgeoisie.* New York: Free Press.

Freeman, S. G. (2004, May 16). Still separate: Still unequal. *New York Times.* Retrieved August 14, 2008, from http://query.nytimes.com/gst/fullpage.html?res=9C04E1D71F3DF935A25756C0A9629C8B63

Gay, G. (1997). Educational equity for students of color. In J. A. Banks & C. A. M. Banks (Eds.), *Multicultural education: Issues and perspectives* (3rd ed.; pp. 195–228). Needham Heights, MA: Allyn & Bacon.

Giddings, P. (1984). *When and where I enter: The impact of Black women or race and sex in America.* New York: Morrow.

Glaser, B. G., & Strauss, A. L. (1967). *The discovery of grounded theory.* Chicago: Aldine.

Goldring, E. B., & Rallis, S. F. (1993). *Principals of dynamic schools: Taking charge of change.* Newbury Park, CA: Corwin.

Goldring, E. B., & Smrekar, C. (1995). *Parental Choice: Consequences for families, schools, and communities.* Technical Summary Report to the Spencer Foundation.

Gordon, J. (2005). In search of educators of color: If we make a more positive experience for students of color, they'll be more likely to continue with their education, and perhaps select teaching as a profession. *Leadership, 35*(2), 30–35.

Hale, J. (2001). *Learning while Black: Creating educational excellence for African American children.* Baltimore, MD: Johns Hopkins University Press.

Hall, P. (1951). Negroes ask for equal educational facilities. In H. Aptheker (Ed.), *A documentary history of the Negro people in the United States.* New York: Citadel. (Original work published 1987)

Haney, J. E. (1978). The effect of the *Brown* decision on Black educators. *Journal of Negro Education, 47*(1), 88–95.

Harding, V. (1981). *There is a river: The Black struggle for freedom in America.* New York: Harcourt Brace Jovanovich.

Harris, C. I. (1993). Whiteness as property. *Harvard Law Review, 106,* 1707–1791.

Heath, S. B., & McLaughlin, M. W. (1987). A child resource policy: Moving beyond dependence on school and family. *Phi Delta Kappan, 68,* 576–580.

Henig, J. R., Hula, R. C., Orr, M., & Pedescleaux, D. S. (1999). *Race, politics, and the challenge of urban education.* Princeton, NJ: Princeton University Press.

Hill, K. (2003, February 24). Desegregation plan supported: Decatur activists seek racial mix in public school. *Atlanta Journal and Constitution,* p. 3C.

Hill-Collins, P. (2000). *Black feminist thought: Knowledge, consciousness, and the politics of empowerment* (2nd ed.). New York: Routledge.

Hill-Collins, P. (2004). *Black sexual politics: African Americans, gender, and the new racism.* New York: Routledge.

Hilliard, A. G., III. (2003). No mystery: Closing the achievement gap between Africans and excellence. In T. Perry, C. Steele, & A. G. Hilliard III (Eds.), *Young, gifted, and Black: Promoting high achievement among African American students* (pp. 131–165). Boston: Beacon.

Holmes, B. (Ed.). (1998). *The status of Black Atlanta 1998.* Atlanta: Southern Center for Studies in Public Policy, Clark Atlanta University.

Honora, D. (2003). Urban African American adolescents and school identification. *Urban Education, 38*(1), 58–76.

hooks, b. (1996). *Bone Black: Memories of girlhood.* New York: Henry Holt.

Hurston, Z. N. (1955, August 11). Court order can't make the races mix. *Orlando Sentinel.* Retrieved September 29, 2008, from http://www.teachingamericanhistory .org/library/index.asp?document=643

Ingersoll, R. M. (2002). Holes in the teacher supply bucket. *School Administrator, 59*(3), 42–43.

Ingram, M., Wolfe, R. B., & Lieberman, J. M. (2007). The role of parents in high-achieving schools serving low-income, at-risk populations. *Education and Urban Society, 39*(4), 479–497.

Irons, P. (2002). *Jim Crow's children: The broken promise of the* Brown *decision.* New York: Penguin.

Irvine, J. J. (1990). *Black students and school failure: Policies, practices, and prescriptions.* New York: Praeger.

Irvine, J. J. (1999a, March). *The education of children whose nightmares occur both night and day.* The Fourth Distinguished Faculty Lecture, Emory University, Atlanta.

Irvine, J. J. (1999b). Preparing teachers for urban classrooms. *Black Issues in Higher Education, 16*(20), 30–32.

Irvine, R., & Irvine, J. J. (1983). The impact of the desegregation process on the education of Black students: Key variables. *Journal of Negro Education, 52,* 410–422.

Jargowsky, P. (1994). Ghetto poverty among Blacks in the 1980s. *Journal of Policy Analysis and Management, 13*, 288–310.

Johnson, C. S. (1954). Some significant social and educational implications of the United States Supreme Court Decision. *Journal of Negro Education, 33*, 368–369.

Jones, A. (1993). *Wade in the water: The wisdom of the spirituals.* Maryknoll, NY: Orbis.

Jones, F. (1981). *A traditional model of educational excellence.* Washington, DC: Howard University Press.

Jones, N. A., & Jackson, J. S. (2001). The demographic profiles of African Americans, 1970–71 to 2000–01. Retrieved November 9, 2003, from http://www .careerday.com/issues/30thAnn/demographic2001–30th.shtml

Jordan, S., & Yeomans, D. (1995). Critical ethnography: Problems in contemporary theory and practice. *British Journal of Sociology of Education, 16*(3), 389–408.

Karenga, M. (1993). *Introduction to Black studies* (2nd ed.). Los Angeles: University of Sankore Press.

King, J. E. (1991). Unfinished business: Black student alienation and Black teachers' emancipatory pedagogy. In M. Foster (Ed.), *Readings on equal education: Qualitative investigations into schools and schooling* (pp. 245–271). New York: AMS.

King, S. H. (1993). The limited presence of African American teachers. *Review of Educational Research, 63*(2), 115–149.

Klarman, M. (2002). Brown v. Board of Education: *Law or Politics?* (Research paper No. 02–11). University of Virginia School of Law, Public Law and Legal Theory Research Paper Series. Retrieved August 7, 2003, from http://ssrn.com/ abstract_id=353361.

Kozol, J. (1991). *Savage inequalities.* New York: Crown.

Kozol, J. (2005). *The shame of the nation: The restoration of apartheid schooling in America.* New York: Crown.

Ladson-Billings, G. (1994). *The dreamkeepers: Successful teachers of African American children.* San Francisco: Jossey-Bass.

Ladson-Billings, G. (2004). Landing on the wrong note: The price we paid for *Brown. Educational Researcher, 33*(7), 3–13.

Lareau, A. (2003). *Unequal childhoods: Class, race, and family life.* Berkeley, CA: University of California Press.

Lareau, A., & Horvat, E. M. (1999). Moments of social inclusion and exclusion: Race, class, and cultural capital in family-school relationships. *Sociology of education, 72*(1), 37–53.

Lee, C. D. (1993). *Signifying as a scaffold for literary interpretation: The pedagogical implications of an African American discourse genre* (Research Report Series). Urbana, IL: National Council of Teachers of English.

Lee, C. D. (1995). A culturally based cognitive apprenticeship: Teaching African American high school students skills in literary interpretation. *Reading Research Quarterly, 30*(4), 608–631.

Lee, E., Menkart, D., & Okazawa-Rey, M. (Eds.). (1998). *Beyond heroes and holidays: A practical guide to K–12 anti-racist, multicultural education and staff development* (pp. 79–82). Washington, DC: Network of Educators on the Americas.

Lemann, N. (1991). *The promised land: The Great Black Migration and how it changed America.* New York: Knopf.

Liddell v. Board of Education of the City of St. Louis, 469 F. Supp. 1387 (Consent Judgment and Decree), (E.D. Mo. 1975).

Liddell v. Board of Education of the City of St. Louis. 469 F. Supp. 1304 (E.D. Mo. 1979).

Liddell v. St. Louis Board of Education, 72C 100(1). Consent Judgment and Decree. U.S. District Court, Eastern District of Missouri (1975).

Lightfoot, S. L. (1983). *The good high school: Portraits of character and culture.* New York: Basic Books.

Lincoln, C. E., & Mamiya, L. H. (1990). *The Black church in the African American experience.* Durham, NC: Duke University Press.

Loder, T. L. (2002). *On women becoming and being principals: Pathways, patterns, & personal accounts.* Unpublished doctoral dissertation, Northwestern University, Evanston.

Loder-Jackson, T. L. (in press). Mary McLeod Bethune. In K. Lomotey (Ed.), *Encyclopedia of African American education.* Thousand Oaks, CA: Sage.

Logan, J., & Deane, G. (2003). Black diversity in metropolitan America. Retrieved August 10, 2008, from http://mumford1.dyndns.org/cen2000/report.html

Lomotey, K. (1989). *African American principals: School leadership and success.* New York: Greenwood.

Lucas, S. R. (1999). *Tracking inequality: Stratification and mobility in American high schools.* New York: Teachers College Press.

Lucas, S. R., & Berends, M. (2007). Race and track location in U.S. public schools. *Research in Social Stratification and Mobility, 25,* 187–269.

Lynn, M. (1999). Toward a critical race pedagogy: A research note. *Urban Education, 33*(5), 606–626.

Mannies, J. (1993, September, 27). Mayor wants to end school busing: City neighborhood suffering, he says. *St. Louis Post-Dispatch,* p. 1A.

Massey, D. S. (1990). American apartheid: Segregation and the making of the underclass. *American Journal of Sociology, 96*(2), 329–357.

Massey, D. S., & Eggers, M. L. (1990). The ecology of inequality: Minorities and the concentration of poverty, 1970–1980. *American Journal of Sociology, 95*(5), 1153.

McCluskey, A. T., & Smith, E. M. (1999). *Mary McLeod Bethune: Building a better world, essays and selected documents.* Bloomington: Indiana University Press.

McNeil, L. M. (1987). Exit, voice, and community: Magnet teachers' responses to standardization. *Educational Policy, 1*(1): 93–113.

Meier, K., Stewart, J., & England, R. E. (1989). *Race, class, and education: The politics of second-generation discrimination.* Madison: University of Wisconsin Press.

Merriam, S. B. (1988). *Case study research in education: A qualitative approach.* San Francisco: Jossey-Bass.

Metz, M. H. (1986). *Different by design: The context and character of three magnet schools.* New York: Routledge & Kegan.

Mickelson, R. A. (2001). Subverting *Swann:* First- and second-generation segregation in Charlotte, North Carolina. *American Educational Research Journal, 38*(2), 215–252.

Miles, M. B., & Huberman, A. M. (1984). *Qualitative data analysis: A sourcebook of new methods.* Beverly Hills, CA: Sage.

Milner, H. R. (2007). Race, culture, and researcher positionality: Working through dangers seen, unseen, and unforeseen. *Educational Researcher, 37*(7), 388–400.

Missouri v. Jenkins, 515 U.S. 70 (1995).

Monroe, C. R. (2005). Why are "bad boys" always Black? Causes of disproportionality in school discipline and recommendations for change. *The Clearing House, 79*(1), 45–50.

Moore, D., & Davenport, S. (1989).*The new improved sorting machine: Concerning school choice.* Chicago: Designs for Change.

Morrell, E., & Duncan-Andrade, J. M. R. (2002). Promoting academic literacy with urban youth through engaging Hip-Hop culture. *English Journal, 91*(6), 88–92.

Morris, J. E. (1997). *Voluntary desegregation in St. Louis, Missouri: Impact on partnerships among schools, African-American families, and communities.* Unpublished doctoral dissertation, Vanderbilt University, Nashville, TN.

Morris, J. E. (1999). A pillar of strength: An African American school's communal bonds with families and communities since *Brown. Urban Education, 33*(5), 584–605.

Morris, J. E. (2001). Malcolm X's critique of the education of Black people. *Western Journal of Black Studies, 25*(2), 126–135.

Morris, J. E. (2002). African-American students and gifted education: The politics of race and culture. *Roeper Review, 24*(2), 59–62.

Morris, J. E. (2003). What does Africa have to do with being African American: A micro-ethnography of identity in an urban middle school classroom. *Anthropology & Education Quarterly, 34*(3), 255–276.

Morris, J. E. (2004). Can anything good come from Nazareth? Race, class, and African-American schooling and community in the urban South and Midwest. *American Educational Research Journal, 41(1),* 69–112.

Morris, J. E., & Fuller, R. (2007, April). *Perceptions of the achievement gap: High achieving black college students reflect on their high school experiences.* Paper presented at the American Educational Research Association annual meeting, Chicago.

Morris, J. E., & Goldring, E. B. (1999). Are magnet schools more equitable? An analysis of the disciplinary rates of African American and White students in Cincinnati magnet and nonmagnet schools. *Equity & Excellence in Education, 32*(3), 59–65.

Morris, V. G., & Morris, C. L. (2002). *The price they paid: Desegregation in an African American community.* New York: Teachers College Press.

National Center for Education Statistics. (2003). *The condition of education.* Washington, DC: U.S. Department of Education.

National Center for Education Statistics. (2008). *The condition of education: Indicator 30, concentration of public school enrollment by locale and race/ethnicity,* Table

30–1. Washington, DC: Author. Retrieved September 24, 2008, from http://nces.ed.gov/programs/coe/list/i4.asp

National Education Association. (2003). *National teacher day spotlights key issues facing profession: NEA addresses top five teaching trends and outlines "Portrait of American Teacher."* Retrieved June 17, 2008, from http://www.nea.org/newsreleases/2006/nr060502.html

Noblit, G. W., & Hare, R. D. (1988). *Meta-ethnography: Synthesizing qualitative studies.* Newbury Park, CA: Sage.

Oakes, J. (1985). *Keeping track: How schools structure inequality.* New Haven, CT: Yale University Press.

Ogbu, J. U. (1978). *Minority education and caste: The American system in cross-cultural perspective.* New York: Academic Press.

Ogbu, J. U. (1990). Overcoming racial barriers to equal access. In J. I. Goodlad & P. Keating (Eds.), *Access to knowledge: An agenda for our nation's schools* (pp. 58–89). New York: The College Board.

Ogbu, J. U. (2003). *Black American students in an affluent suburb: A study of academic disengagement.* Mahwah, NJ: Erlbaum.

Ogletree, C. J. (2004). *All deliberate speed: Reflections on the first half-century of* Brown v. Board of Education. New York: W.W. Norton.

Orfield, G., & Ashkinaze, C. (1991). *The closing door: Conservative policy and Black opportunity.* Chicago: University of Chicago Press.

Orfield, G., Eaton, S. E., & the Harvard Project on School Desegregation. (Eds.). (1996). *Dismantling desegregation: The quiet reversal of* Brown v. Board of Education. New York: New Press.

Orfield, G., & Lee, C. (2007). Historic reversals, accelerating resegregation, and the need for new integration strategies: A report of the Civil Rights Project/Provecto Derechos Civiles. UCLA. http://www.civilrightsproject.ucla.edu/research/deseg/reverals_reseg_need.pdf. Website accessed on 6/20/2008

Orr, M. (1999). *Black social capital: The politics of school reform in Baltimore, 1986–1998.* Lawrence: University Press of Kansas.

Painter, N. E. (2002). *Southern history across the color line.* Chapel-Hill: University of North Carolina Press.

Paley, V. G. (1989). *White teacher.* Cambridge, MA: Harvard University Press.

Parents Involved in Community Schools v Seattle School District No. 1 et al., decided with Meredith v. Jefferson County Board of Education et al., [Seattle/Louisville case], 551 U.S. (2007).

Patterson, J. T. (2001). *Brown v. Board of Education: A civil rights milestone and its troubled legacy.* New York: Oxford University Press.

Pattillo-McCoy, M. (1999). *Black picket fences: Privilege and peril among the Black middle class.* Chicago: University of Chicago Press.

Perry, T. (2003). Up from the parched earth: Toward a theory of African American achievement. In T. Perry, C. Steele, & A. G. Hilliard III (Eds.), *Young, gifted, and Black: Promoting high achievement among African American students* (pp. 1–10). Boston: Beacon.

Philipsen, M. (1994). The second promise of *Brown. The Urban Review, 26*(4), 257–272.

Powell, J. A., Jeffries, H. K., Newhart, D. W., & Stiens, E. (2006). Towards a transformative view of race: The crisis and opportunity of Katrina. In C. Hartman & G. D. Squires (Eds.), *There is no such thing as a natural disaster: Race, class, and Hurricane Katrina* (pp. 59–84). New York: Routledge.

Quillian, L. (1999). Migration patterns and the growth of high-poverty neighborhoods, 1970–1990. *American Journal of Sociology, 105*, 1–37.

Raywid, M. A. (1989). *The case for public schools of choice.* Bloomington, IN: Phi Delta Kappa Educational Foundation.

Reitzug, U. C., & Patterson, J. (1998). "I'm not going to lose you!" Empowerment through caring in an urban principal's practice with students. *Urban Education, 33*(2), 150–181.

Roberts v. City of Boston, 59 Mass (5 Cush), 198, 201–204 (1850).

Rothstein, R. (2004). *Class and schools: Using social, economic, and educational reform to close the Black–White achievement gap.* New York: Teachers College Press.

Royster, D. (2003). *Race and the invisible hand: How White networks exclude Black men from blue-collar jobs.* Berkeley: University of California Press.

Rubovitz, C. P., & Maehr, M. (1973). Pygmalion Black and White. *Journal of Personality and Social Psychology, 25*, 210–218.

Sanders, M. G. (2008). How parent liaisons can help bridge the home-school gap. *Journal of Educational Research, 101*(5), 287–298.

Savage, C. J. (1998). *From Claiborne Institute to Natchez High School: The history of African American education in Williamson County, Tennessee, 1890–1967.* Unpublished Ed.D. Dissertation, Peabody College of Vanderbilt University, Nashville, TN.

Scheurich, J. J. (1998). Highly successful and loving, public elementary schools populated mainly by low-SES children of color. *Urban Education, 23*(4), 451–491.

Scheurich, J. J., & Young, M. D. (1997). Coloring epistemologies: Are our research epistemologies racially biased? *Educational Researcher, 25*(4), 4–15.

Sebring, P. B., & Bryk, A. S. (2000). School leadership and the bottom line in Chicago. *Phi Delta Kappan, 81*(6), 440–443.

Segall, A. (2001). Critical ethnography and the invocation of voice: From the field/ in the field—single exposure/double standard? *International Journal of Qualitative Studies in Education, 14*(4), 579–592.

Serwatka, T. S., Deering, S., & Grant, P. (1995). Disproportionate representation of African Americans in emotionally handicapped classes. *Journal of Black Studies, 25*, 492–506.

Shaw, C. (1966). *The Jack-Roller: A delinquent boy's own story.* Chicago: University of Chicago Press.

Shelley v. Kramer, 334 U.S. 1 (1948).

Shelton, S. (2001). Gentrification takes toll on poor, elderly: Longtimers often must sell. *Atlanta Journal and Constitution*, p. F5.

Shujaa, M. J., & Afrik, H. (1996). School desegregation, the politics of culture, and the Council of Independent Black Institutions. In M. J. Shujaa (Ed.), *Beyond desegregation: The politics of quality in African American schooling* (pp. 253–268). Thousand Oaks, CA: Corwin.

Siddle Walker, E. V. (1996). *Their highest potential: An African American school community in the segregated South.* Chapel Hill: University of North Carolina Press.

Siddle Walker, E. V. (2000). Valued segregated schools for African American children in the South, 1935–1969: A review of common themes and characteristics. *Review of Educational Research, 70,* 253–286.

Sjoquist, D. L. (2000). (Ed.). *The Atlanta paradox.* New York: Russell Sage Foundation.

Smith, P. (1999). Our children's burden: The many-headed hydra of the educational disenfranchisement of Black children. *Howard Law Journal, 42*(2), 133–239.

Smrekar, C., & Goldring, E. B. (1999). *School choice in urban America: Magnet schools and the pursuit of equity.* New York: Teachers College Press.

Southern Education Foundation. (2003). *A new majority: Low-income students in the South's public schools.* Retrieved April 17, 2008, from http://www.sefatl.org/showTeaser.asp?did=542

Stanford, G. C. (1997). Successful pedagogy in urban schools: Perspectives of four African American teachers. *Journal of Education for Students Placed at Risk, 2*(2), 107–119.

Stewart, J. B. (1990). Back to basics: The significance of Du Bois's and Frazier's contributions for contemporary research on Black families. In H. E. Cheatham & J. B. Stewart (Eds.), *Black families: Interdisciplinary perspectives.* New Brunswick, NJ: Transaction.

Stone, C. N. (1989). *Regime politics: Governing Atlanta, 1946–1988.* Lawrence: University Press of Kansas.

Street, P. (2005). *Segregated schools: Educational apartheid in post–civil rights America.* New York: Routledge.

Tate, W. F. (1997). Critical race theory and education: History, theory, and implications. In Michael W. Apple (Ed.), *Review of research in education* (pp. 195–247). Washington, DC: American Educational Research Association.

Tatum, B. D. (1997). *Why are all the Black kids sitting together in the cafeteria? And other conversations about race.* New York: Basic Books.

Thernstrom, A., & Thernstrom, S. (2003). *No excuses: Closing the racial gap in learning.* New York: Simon & Schuster.

Tillman, L. C. (2002). Culturally sensitive research approaches: An African American perspective. *Educational Researcher, 31*(9), 3–12.

Tyson, K., Darity, W., Jr., & Castellino, D. (2005). It's not a Black thing: Understanding the burden of acting White and other dilemmas of high achievement. *American Sociological Review, 70*(4), 582–605.

United Negro College Fund. (2001). *Just the facts: Educators for the new millennium.* Washington, DC: Frederick Patterson Research Institute.

U.S. Census Bureau. (1990). Census 1990. Washington, DC: Author.

U.S. Census Bureau. (2000). Census 2000. Washington, DC: Author.

U.S. Census Bureau. (2002). *Annual demographic supplement to the March 2002 current population survey.* Washington, DC: Author.

U.S. Census Bureau. (2004a). *American community survey.* Washington, DC: Author.

U.S. Census Bureau. (2004b). *Current population survey, 2004 annual social and economic supplement.* Washington, DC: Author.

U.S. Census Bureau. (2005). *American housing survey.* Washington, DC: Author.

U.S. Department of Education, National Center for Education Statistics. (2001–2002). Common core of data.

U.S. Department of Education, National Center for Education Statistics. (2008). Common core of data.

Wells, A. S., & Crain, R. L. (1997). *Stepping over the color line: African American students in White suburban schools.* New Haven, CT: Yale University Press.

Wells, A. S., Holme, J. J., Atanda, A. K., & Revilla, A. T. (2005). Tackling racial segregation one policy at a time: Why school desegregation only went so far. *Teachers College Record, 107*(9) 2141–2177.

West, C. (1982). *Prophesy deliverance! An Afro-American revolutionary Christianity.* Philadelphia: Westminster.

West, C. (1988). *Prophetic fragments.* Grand Rapids, MI: Eerdmans.

Williams, H. A. (2005). *Self-taught: African American education in slavery and freedom.* Chapel Hill, NC: University of North Carolina Press.

Willie, C. V., Reddick, R. J., & Brown, R. (2006). *The Black college mystique.* Lanham, ND: Rowman & Littlefield.

Wilson, W. J. (1987). *The truly disadvantaged: The inner city, the underclass, and public policy.* Chicago: University of Chicago Press.

Wilson, W. J. (1996). *When work disappears: The world of the new urban poor.* New York: Knopf.

Wright, J. A. (1994). *Discovering African American St. Louis: A guide to historic sites.* St. Louis: Missouri Historical Society Press.

Yin, R. K. (1989). *Case study research: Design and methods.* Newbury Park, CA: Sage.

Zuberi, T. (2004). W. E. B. DuBois's sociology: The Philadelphia Negro and social science. *Annals of the American Academy of Political and Social Science, 595*(1), 146–156.

Index

About the Author

Dr. Jerome E. Morris is an associate professor in the College of Education and director of the Race, Class, Place and Outcomes Research Group in the Institute for Behavioral Research (where he also serves as a research fellow) at the University of Georgia. His research and teaching focus on the sociology and anthropology of education and examine the intersection of race, social class, gender, and immigrant status with social and educational policies. He has published extensively in leading research journals, such as the *American Educational Research Journal, Teachers College Record, Anthropology and Education*, and *Educational Researcher*. With major funding from the Spencer Foundation in Chicago, he is presently leading a longitudinal study of how identity, social class status, and geographical context influence adolescents' educational experiences and achievement outcomes in Black suburbia in the U.S. South.